D1004044

The Open Minded Tarot:
A Practical Guide

Kate Ross

Vodnik Publishing

Copyright © 2012 Vodnik Publishing
All rights reserved.

ISBN-978-0-9877677-0-7

TABLE OF CONTENTS

FOREWORD

I believe that reading tarot is far more interesting and complex than simply reading one card at a time and reporting what they mean. *You will take a trip over the ocean; you will meet a handsome stranger; you will fall into some money....* These are stock phrases that are used and frankly, they're a bit ridiculous. It brings to mind some swooning old woman with a crystal ball and a scarf on her head. It doesn't provoke dialogue and it doesn't make people feel better about their lives.

My goal when I read for people is to have them leave feeling better than when they came to me. Even if the reading is not entirely positive, I really do strive to have people walk away from my table feeling like they are in control of their lives and the decisions they make; that they will always have a choice to make and that even in times of strife they can maintain their dignity and look forward to better times.

This is what I would like to communicate to you. I believe that reading tarot is an art, the art of a dialogue between two people. It's the art of empowerment. It's the art of living consciously. We are not pawns; we can make decisions and effect real and meaningful change in our own lives on a daily basis. Though it makes no sense to be told what do to by pieces of paper, it does make sense to use the cards to help clarify issues and create strategies for problem solving.

I bought my first deck when I was eighteen years old and read a great deal and learned as much as I could. I was always too shy to read for anyone else and just used the cards on my own, never really having any idea what they meant and sometimes feeling vaguely uneasy about seeing a card that I thought might have a negative meaning. Years later I was fortunate enough to apprentice with a woman who was a professional reader and all the studying I had done before solidified. I learned the importance of *how* to talk to a Querent and what to say when delicate or personal topics came up. I highly recommend that if at all possible, you find someone who will help you learn. Learning from a book is one thing, but learning from an experienced reader and watching a reading in action is quite another.

I've never been very comfortable taking money from people. I find it awkward. I read not to earn money but out of a genuine desire to help people. I'll read for anyone and though I do insist that as tradition dictates, money changes hands, I ask for a coin as a token. I keep a jar of coins in my kitchen and tell people to take out a coin and pay me if they haven't got one with them. I'm not and never have been interested in taking people's money doing this. I did read for money for a brief period, years ago, but it never felt right to me. I have a job to put food on the table and tarot is what I do to feed my soul.

That being said, there are some people who earn their living at reading cards. This is not a bad thing. What I don't agree with is when people assert that they are psychic when they are not, or ask for immense sums of money to remove "bad energy", do spells on behalf of their clients etc.

I'm not a psychic and to be honest, I'm uncomfortable with the term. I don't pretend to know the future because I see the future as largely unknowable and that's what makes it wonderful. I also know that it doesn't take a psychic to look at a big black cloud on the horizon and predict a storm. I'm reasonably good at reading people, expressions, body language etc. but I get fooled just like everybody else. I'm not going to wrap myself up in a mystic cloak to sell this book. It's true that sometimes I have a hunch or a feeling about things but where that feeling comes from I really couldn't say. Maybe I'm responding to flashes of body language; maybe I'm picking up on subtle hints that people give off. Sometimes I'm right and sometimes I'm wrong.

I don't believe that the tarot is about psychic experience. For me, the tarot is an amazing tool to stimulate dialogue and help people decide which path they want to take. It's not a parlour game, it's not evil; it's not going to tell anyone anything about their own life they don't already know on some level.

There is no part of our lives that is completely compartmentalised. Your home life affects your work; your work affects your health; your health affects everything. I believe it's impossible to read the tarot one card at a time and not see how each card affects the cards around it. By learning to think laterally, that is, to see the cards as they are in relation to each other, you will deepen your experience and give richer, more meaningful readings. Seeing a spread as a flow of information instead of individual and unconnected pieces of information is far more fascinating and so much truer to real life. When we suffer or have joy in one part of our lives, it naturally affects everything else. Many of the books I have read over the years give the meanings of the cards but no real life examples of how to apply those meanings. Reading a book is one thing, but having a real live person in front of you (even if you're reading only for yourself) and not having any idea what the cards mean or how they go together is largely useless, in my opinion. This book will teach you not only how to interpret the cards, but how to actually read for another person, which are two different things entirely. Reading for a person is a dialogue. In order to put that dialogue into play, you need to be armed with not only the meanings of the cards but the ways in which to interpret the surrounding cards and how to actually deliver the news to the Querent diplomatically and honestly. Also available, The Open Minded Tarot Workbook is an exercise book to help sharpen your skills and make connections between the various cards and to aid in learning to interpret combinations.

Choosing a deck that suits you is important if you are new to Tarot and unsure of what you are doing. I would suggest that the Rider-Waite deck is excellent to start with as the illustrations on each card are full of symbolism, making it easier to read than other more abstract decks. You will notice that I have not included pictorial representations of each card in this book. Since there are so many types of decks available, I feel it will be more helpful for you, the Reader, to use your own deck in tandem with this book, rather than looking at illustrations which may differ from your own deck and which could cause confusion.

I wish you the best of luck in your journey and hope it will be rewarding and satisfying.

Kate Ross

THE TAROT: BACKGROUND AND HELPFUL INFORMATION

The tarot was first used about 500 years ago, most probably in central Italy and used at first as a card game called Tarocchi, which is still played today. Many years ago, before printing presses and cheap paper, decks were very expensive. They were hand-painted and commissioned by only the wealthiest families. It is likely that the cards were not originally used for divination but for playing card games. The "fortune telling" properties of the tarot came later.

The best way to begin to explain the tarot is probably by explaining what I believe it isn't. It isn't a spooky way to communicate with dark forces. In my opinion, it isn't antireligious or "against God" (whatever that means). It's not going to tell you for 100% certain what the future will hold because nobody knows what the future will hold. Fortune-telling is illegal in a lot of places as it can lend itself to sham readers and fraud. It is particularly wrong to take advantage of gullible, vulnerable people by convincing them that they need cards to help them make decisions in their lives.

I believe that the tarot is an excellent way of pinpointing the problems and challenges faced by all of us. Since each card (and the combinations of the cards around it) can have multiple meanings, any one of these cards can be applicable to your life at any particular moment. It's up to you if you feel that the appearance of any particular card is mystical or brought on by some kind of unseen force or simply the result of a random shuffle. Either way, using the tarot is an excellent way of provoking dialogue, clarifying your thoughts or opinions on a subject, helping to clear away the fog of indecision and assisting in making plans.

Take care however, that you do **not** use the tarot to make decisions for you. These are cards, pieces of paper, and though they are helpful tools, they cannot tell you what to do or how to live your life. Remember that every decision you make will affect the way you live your life, and that turning left instead of right one day can make all the difference. You are in control, no one else.

WHAT IS A QUERENT?

A Querent is the person for whom the reading is done. The name comes from "query" which means "question". The Querent could be a client, a friend or even yourself. The Reader is the person reading the cards.

Remember that information relayed in the cards could be a message about something the Querent has done or something another person has done to the Querent. It could be a situation the Querent finds themselves in. The Querent may be the victim or the perpetrator of any misfortunes in their lives.

It is very important to deal with the Querent in an ethical and honest manner. If you do not understand how a particular card applies to a Querent's life, say so. Never invent anything in order to look like you know what you're talking about. Always tell the truth about what you see in the cards. Do not exaggerate. Remember, someone has trusted you with the details of their life, reward their trust accordingly.

TRADITIONS

Here are some traditions and helpful hints about reading the tarot.

Always keep your deck either wrapped in a white or light coloured silk scarf or in a box made of wood. Some people say that natural fabric or wood keeps away bad vibrations.

Always count the cards before you begin reading to be sure you haven't lost any cards, thus compromising the integrity of the deck.

Some people say you should buy your own deck, others say the deck needs to be bought for you. I believe it's up to you, just so long as you have a deck you can work with.

Some people believe you should not read under your real name. This goes back to the time when reading tarot was punishable by law. On one hand, it does protect your privacy. On the other hand, this kind of thing can lend itself to fraud. Many readers use their first names only.

Other than asking the Querent to shuffle the cards at the beginning of a reading, don't let other people handle your cards. If you want to show people the tarot in a more casual way, have another deck handy (one that you don't use in readings) and let people look through that.

Don't read out in the open or in semi-public places. This is partly out of respect, the tarot isn't a parlour game, and partly it hails back to the times when "fortune telling" was a punishable offence. Some people say you should never let direct sunlight or moonlight fall on your cards. Essentially, read indoors and in private.

Don't read for a Querent in front of other people; especially don't read for husbands in front of wives and vice versa. This might seem strange, but if you think about some of the personal things that come up during readings, you can see how people might not want to discuss personal matters in front of other people. For example, imagine how awkward this would be: "There's a woman in your life who is domineering and unstable and she creates a great deal of trouble for you." "Oh yes, that's my mother-in-law. That's your mother, isn't it, Ted?"

Don't read for the same person twice in one day. It's considered disrespectful. Take the answer you've received and think about it and then if you want to do another spread, do it another day.

Be gentle with your deck, don't slam it hard on the table or leave it laying around. If you treat your deck gently, it will treat you gently too.

If a card "jumps" the deck when the Querent is shuffling (falls out of the deck), don't put it back in the deck with all the other cards. Lay it aside and read it at the end. That card "jumped" out because it has a special significance.

Don't read for children unless they understand how the tarot can be used as a problem-solving tool. They're more likely to be influenced and to believe that fate has decided something for them because the cards will it to be so. If they get Death or the Tower, they might become frightened.

Assure the Querent that you treat a reading like a confessional. It's completely private and that you won't be repeating to others what is discussed. Then, don't discuss it.

Wear a coin on your person in the form of a necklace, earrings, or bracelet. In a pinch, I have tucked a coin into the cuff of my sleeve and then rolled it up. It brings good luck to the Querent. Tell them they have to pay you, even a nickel. Money has to change hands, even if you're just reading for fun. In the beginning, when you're practicing, read for everyone you know. (If they want you to!) Keep a bunch of pennies in a jar, tell them to take one out and pay you.

ABOUT THE TAROT DECK

The traditional tarot is generally made up of seventy-eight cards. Fifty-six of these cards are the Minor Arcana, and twenty-two make up the Major Arcana. "Arcana" comes from the Latin word which means "secrets", although I personally do not believe the tarot can tell you anything about your life that you don't already know.

THE MINOR ARCANA

The Minor Arcana is made up of four suits which correspond to the suits in a regular deck of playing cards. They are:

Swords (spades),
Swords can refer to stress, conflict, sexual issues, rumour, gossip, and mental clarity.

Wands (clubs),
Wands can refer to intellectual issues with a work or educational focus, and energy.

Coins (also called Pentacles) (diamonds),
Coins can refer to health / monetary issues.

Cups (hearts),
Cups can refer to emotional issues and relationships.

Minor Arcana cards tend to appear in a spread when dealing with the issues of daily life. Each of the four suits deals with the various parts of our lives such as health, finances, love and relationships, conflict etc.

The Minor Arcana includes Pages, Knights, Queens and Kings, also known as "Court Cards" which can be read as individuals in the Querent's life (or the Querent herself), situations, messages or personal characteristics.

THE MAJOR ARCANA

Generally speaking, Major Arcana cards tend to appear when the Querent is undergoing a bigger shift than what they encounter in their normal, everyday life. These changes can be a shift in mentality, spirituality; a literal move from one home to another, job changes, and significant life changes such as births, deaths, the start or end of relationships, serious problems or periods of reward and happiness.

The twenty-two cards of the Major Arcana can represent the experiences we must have and the types of people we must encounter in order to become well-rounded adults. Growing up is a journey. We start from innocence and naiveté and then (hopefully) move on, acquiring wisdom and experience on the way. Cynicism and a rigid attitude cloud our judgement both as Querents and as readers.

The Major Arcana begins at 0 and finishes at 21. The first card is the Fool. This does not necessarily indicate a foolish person, but can indicate someone innocent and unlearned. The number used to describe the state of being new at something is zero; we start from nothing and make our way through this world. The Major Arcana are as follows:

0	the Fool
1	the Magician
2	the High Priestess

(in some decks she is referred to as "the Papess")

3	the Empress
4	the Emperor
5	the Hierophant

(in some decks he is referred to as the Pope)

6	the Lovers
7	the Chariot
8	Justice
9	the Hermit
10	the Wheel of Fortune
11	Strength
12	Hanged Man
13	Death
14	Temperance
15	the Devil
16	the Tower

(in some decks it is referred to as 'Maison Dieu')

17	the Star
18	the Moon
19	the Sun
20	Judgement
21	the World

DIGNIFIED VS. ILL DIGNIFIED (REVERSED) CARDS

Cards are shuffled and then laid down on the table face up. If the card is turned the "right" way (bottom and top being in the right direction) they are referred to as "Dignified". If the card is "upside down", (top and bottom are reversed) they are referred to as "Ill Dignified" or "reversed".

Some readers do not make a differentiation between cards which are right-side up (Dignified) and cards which are reversed (Ill Dignified). I was taught and I do believe that a reversed card is, in fact, different from the meaning of a dignified card. This can cause some confusion. A reversed card can either be an intensification of the meaning of the card or it can mean a smaller problem or a delay. For example:

the Tower (dignified)
  = Sudden change, calamity, problems.

the Tower (reversed)
  = Enormous sudden change, disastrous consequences, a life completely falling apart.

Or

the Tower (reversed)
  = An inconvenient problem, but nothing you can't deal with. An oncoming problem which can be dealt with or controlled: a delay of the inevitable.

READING TAROT CARDS

There are as many different ways to read and interpret cards as there are readers. None of these ways is inherently good or bad, wrong or right. It is an individual craft which takes years and hard work to master. Here is some information about how to read cards.

LEARNING TO READ CARD COMBINATIONS

The best way to be able to interpret the meaning of a card is to look at the cards surrounding it, and to talk to the Querent and get a sense of their life. Just as every part of your life is connected (your work affects your health, which affects your private life, which affects your work) the cards also affect each other. Reading combinations takes some practice but it will enrich your readings and make them more interesting for both you and the Querent.

You will notice that I often use the phrase "next to" when talking about cards that appear in the same spread. I do not mean to say that a card must be physically to the left or the right of another card in order for it to have an influence. I feel this sort of reading is too rigid and the possibility of losing the thread or the theme of the reading is too great. I simply mean that when certain cards appear in the same spread, they can compliment or enhance each other's meaning, regardless of whether they are physically directly next to one another.

Start by looking at the cards two by two (any more than this can be overwhelming). There are two main ways to see them; 1) Cause and Effect, and 2) Intensifiers or Modifiers.

Cause and Effect

Cause and effect is exactly what it sounds like. One card results in something else. Here are some examples:

The Lovers III Dignified + Three of Swords – here you see the end of a relationship and the resulting emotional tumult. The Three of Swords is a sorrowful card about grieving and loss; it's the effect of a relationship gone sour.

The Three of Coins + Six of Wands –
The Three of Coins speaks about taking pride in your work and applying yourself carefully to a task. The Six of Wands speaks of victory. Therefore, this combination can indicate that careful and diligent work will result in some sort of victory for the Querent.

Intensifiers / Modifiers

Combinations which intensify or modify the result of cards can be a little bit more subtle. Look at these combinations.

Four of Swords III Dignified + Ace of Wands –
The Ace of Wands is about potential action, a new plan to invigorate the life of the Querent. Its power is lessened somewhat by the presence of the Four of Swords, a card that speaks of knowing what it is you're supposed to do but simply not doing it. This

19

combination says that the potential power the Querent has to change his life is being hampered by laziness or fear.

The Tower III Dignified + The World –
The Tower speaks of a sudden and shocking change in the life of the Querent. The World speaks of success being reached at the end of a journey. In this case, it would seem that the change will not be of a catastrophic nature and that it is, in fact, to the Querent's benefit.

Reading combinations takes time and effort. No two readers will see the cards the same way, and that goes doubly for reading combinations. This is not a bad thing. I don't believe in memorising long lists of combinations and spitting out a rote response to the Querent. I prefer the idea of seeing the cards as changeable depending on the situation and the person you are reading for. I also prefer not to dictate to you what combinations mean. In this book, I have given possible interpretations of cards and beneath each interpretation there are a few combinations listed and what they could indicate. **Those combinations aren't meant to be memorised.** These are simply guidelines to give you an idea how one person (namely, me) reads those combinations.

Remember that depending on the situation and the dialogue that you have with the Querent, what works in one situation may not apply in another. The Tarot is a path, and it is your path just as much as it is mine. You must form your own associations and start to see things in your own way.

Each person is unique and though, at heart, our problems might all be similar, our lives, personalities and experiences are not. It stands to reason then, that reading for people requires more than simple rote, automatic responses to the cards you see in front of you.

PRACTICAL INFORMATION ON READING TAROT

Reading tarot is strange in one way because though you'll hear the same thing over and over again (my partner, my job, my education, my kids...) you'll never hear it in the same way twice. You might find that people suddenly think of you as having some kind of wisdom, as though your life has never had any trouble and that you always know the right thing to do. You know something they don't, and that automatically puts you in a position of power and influence. You might find Querents confessing all kinds of things to you and then asking you very sincerely what they should do about it. That's a lot of responsibility and don't be afraid to tell them that you don't have all the answers and that they need to make important decisions on their own.

You'll often find you've got a nervous Querent in front of you. Their hands are clenched, they look down. You can tell they're not comfortable. If this is their first reading, it could be that they feel nervous they're going to get bad news. It could also be that they've been told by some people that this kind of thing is bad and sinful and they will be punished. The best you can do is assure them that this is a conversation, that it's a dialogue using cards that help them to pinpoint problems in their lives and that it's not unholy or satanic in any way. If they really look uncomfortable, tell them directly that they don't have to have a reading if they don't want to. **It's not for everyone, and that's perfectly fine.**

Sometimes people come to a reading and are strangely hostile. It could be that they are scared or nervous or that they want to "debunk" you. I find this odd, to be honest. If you don't believe in this sort of thing, why go out of your way to try it? I've asked questions of Querents and heard "you're the psychic, you tell me". That's the point where I simply say, *"I'm not a psychic. I'm a normal, everyday person, just like you. I can't tell you anything about your life that you don't already know. I don't have any special powers. I'm here to talk to you about your life, about issues you are facing. I can help you by telling you what these cards mean but I can't tell you what to do or what is going to happen to you in the future. I'm not here for that. These cards aren't magic. They're paper. The magic and the power come from inside of you."*

If someone is new to tarot, give them a brief explanation of the deck. Explain that it comes from Italy, it's five hundred years old; that it's made up of seventy-eight cards, fifty-six Minor Arcana and twenty-two Major Arcana. Explain what the difference is between Major and Minor and that the word "Arcana" comes from the Latin word for "secrets". Be sure to explain:

"Of course, these aren't secrets; I can't tell you anything about your life that you don't already know. I don't have a crystal ball, and this isn't about fortune telling."

It may sound silly but it is necessary. You'd be surprised how many people think you "know" their innermost secrets.

You can show the Querent some examples of the Major Arcana; explain quickly that it follows the path of a life journey, of the lessons we all need to learn in order to be well-rounded people. Then, show them a couple of examples of each suit and quickly explain what each suit generally represents. If they understand and have no questions, ask them to shuffle the deck.

Usually by the time you've finished this explanation, the Querent starts to relax; you've taken the "mystery" out of it, not by making it seem like a game but by simplifying it. People are less likely to be afraid of things they understand.

If they have had a reading before and are not afraid of the process yet they are still nervous, it probably indicates that there are some big things going on in their lives. Watch their body language. When you hit a nerve in your explanations of the meanings of the cards, you'll know it immediately. Ask them *"Does that sound familiar to you?"* and then let them describe the situation. Don't be afraid of a little silence. Sometimes people just need a moment to get up the courage to say what they came to say.

Don't be surprised if people begin to cry when you read for them. Have tissues handy. There's a great deal of stress out there and when speaking about personal problems, people will often break down and cry. They might even feel comfortable crying in front of you precisely because they don't know you. If watching other people cry makes you uncomfortable, the only thing I can tell you is get used to it. Give the Querent a tissue, be silent for a moment and then ask them if they want to continue.

"I see this is a difficult time for you, let's try and talk this through and see how we can come up with something to make this load lighter for you."

People get scared when they see what they perceive as being "negative" cards and start thinking they're going to get hit by a bus on their way home. I've seen Querents have a visceral reaction when they see the Death card or the Tower. They feel immediately afraid and think "Oh no, why did I do this?" Assure them immediately that it's not so bad. If you do a reading and it seems that every card you pull is imminent disaster, you'll have to tell the Querent that things are not so rosy. Try something like this:

"It looks as if there's the possibility of (or you are already in) a really challenging period of your life. Things might seem overwhelming and you might feel alone. The important thing to remember is that this situation is not going to last the rest of your life; it's temporary. Every one of these cards that indicate a challenge also has the flip side of a lesson learned, strength gained, wisdom won. You won't be necessarily doing cart-wheels, but know that you're not being given anything you can't handle. You may need to ask for help from time to time, and it's important to remember there's nothing wrong with that. A lot of troubles can be avoided. Nothing is set in stone. You could turn left instead of right on a street one day and that could make all the difference."

Never, under any circumstances, make a pronouncement of doom. **It is irresponsible and abusive to frighten someone.**

In the end, cards are neither good nor bad, they're just cards and they tell a story. If someone is panicked because they think they've got "bad" cards, remind them that this isn't the case. Cards may indicate struggle or stress, but that doesn't mean you're 100% headed for disaster. Trouble can be averted if people plan, think, organise themselves, act accordingly and try to be decent. Most of the trouble we get into is a result of our own behaviour anyway so the tarot can be used to remind us to steer clear of trouble before it starts which is easier than trying to do damage control after the fact.

Always tell the truth about what you see in the cards. Be tactful but direct.

If you see an indicator of sickness, ask the Querent if they enjoy good health, or if they're feeling well. Remind them that they need to take care of their bodies and that they should get regular check-ups.

If you see an indicator that there are problems in a Querent's love life, ask them about their relationships, if all is well. Let them show you how deep they want to get. Your instinct might tell you exactly what the problem is. Ask them how the relationship is progressing, if there have been any changes. You can look at the cards and then say something like:

"It looks like both of you have different ideas about what you want in a relationship." Or:

25

"There's a possibility of some bumps ahead, be sure you're honest with each other."

If they ask you, "Is my husband cheating on me?" You have to tell them clearly and gently that of course a deck of cards can't tell anyone something like that and that the best thing to do is to talk to their partner themselves. You can tell them the cards indicate a lot of emotion, sadness, fear, deception etc, but it wouldn't be right to accuse someone of something as serious as cheating or stealing because a tarot card reader said so.

Most people who come to a tarot reader know what they're coming for. There is often a single source of stress or a problem that they need to discuss and work through. Be sure to ask the Querent what they would like to talk about today, if they have anything particular on their minds. If you get the feeling they are holding back, ask them if there is anything else. Assure them that what they say is held in confidence and that there is no judgement on your part.

If the Querent is the one cheating or doing something incorrect, even if you find what they're doing absolutely repugnant, don't react to it. People don't come to tarot readers to be validated. That's what their friends are for. They come to tarot readers to find out what the future consequences of present actions are. If they are involved in an activity that's immoral or unethical and they aren't complete jerks, they know what they are doing is wrong. In this case, you don't need to say much more than to gently remind them that for every action there is an equal and opposite reaction.

26

Don't be afraid to end a reading if someone is making you uncomfortable. If you hear something that you feel is illegal or dangerous, report it to the police. You're not bound by the same rules as lawyers or priests. Repeating gossip is one thing, but preventing a crime is another thing entirely.

Never promise anything you can't deliver on. Though I believe some people have excellent intuition, I'm not convinced that there are people out there who know the future one hundred percent of the time. There are readers who tell their clients that they will be able to help them with their personal or financial problems. That's a big promise and I suspect it's one that's broken quite frequently.

There are readers who prey on vulnerable people by telling them that for a price, they can "remove bad energy" or cast spells in order to improve the lives of the Querent. Honestly, I feel these people are scam artists and are taking advantage of others and deserve to be prosecuted for fraud.

HOW TO CONDUCT A READING

How do you actually conduct a reading?

First, be sure you have an appropriate space. Obviously you need a table and comfortable chairs. You can decorate if you like. The most important thing is to have a space where people can relax and feel free to speak their minds.

Turn off your phone or let your calls go to voice mail. Turn off the radio and the television. Make sure there are no distractions and that you have privacy.

You can light candles if you like. I usually take a plate and put some salt on it. I put candles on the plate and light them. I was taught that salt keeps bad vibrations away. Whether or not you believe this, it does serve as a reminder that it is better to read the tarot with a clear head and good intentions than to read while feeling negative. No matter how "spiritual" or "practical" you are, most people can agree that you reap what you sow, so it's better to begin with clarity and calm rather than with anger or negativity.

You can light incense, however not everyone likes it, so I would ask the Querent first or light it in another room.

Avoid getting too theatrical. It can turn people off or worse yet, frighten them.

Ask them if they have ever had a reading before. If they haven't, briefly explain to them what the tarot is, its origins, the suits and what they stand for, and the difference between Major and Minor Arcana.

Personally, I see a reading as a dialogue and not as a monologue from the reader, who drones on and on while the Querent absorbs all the information (or tries to). I really do believe that people get more out of a reading if they feel they've participated in it, asked questions, clarified things and talked about their lives. There's something very soothing and healing about just talking about your life. A very good friend of mine says that a lot of times when people are telling you their problems it might be the first time they're hearing the problem out loud. They may have had these issues bottled up inside of them for some time and simply never had the occasion to say it out loud. Hearing your own voice as you talk about your problem is a very powerful thing. As another friend of mine says, you have to name it to tame it.

With this in mind, you can begin.

Make sure you've counted the deck, preferably before the Querent arrives, so that you can be sure that all seventy-eight cards are there. When I count the cards, I put all of them facing in one direction, so that any cards which turn upside-down (Ill Dignified) are due to the Querent shuffling and not due to me or anyone else.

Ask them to "wash the deck". Putting the cards face down on the table, ask the Querent to spread them around and around, generally making a big mess until they feel they've finished, and then ask them to put the deck back together again. Then, ask them to shuffle at least seven times, reminding them to be gentle with the deck. When they have finished shuffling, ask them if they are left or right handed. If they are right handed, ask them to cut the deck into three piles with their left hand. If they are left handed, ask them to use the right hand. I was taught that this is because the opposite hand is more influenced by their true nature. I'm not sure if I believe this, but out of respect for the process, it's simply something I have always done. Then, with the deck in three piles, and still using the opposite hand, ask them to put the deck back together again, any way they like.

Now the deck is "theirs" which simply means that any messages that come from the deck, any topics that come up are directly meant for the Querent and not as a result of any influence on your part, nor from any previous Querents.

Take any cards that may have jumped the deck while the Querent was shuffling and put them aside. Read them at the end.

What spread you should use is entirely up to you. I often use an inverted pyramid beginning with six cards in a horizontal row, five in the row below it and then four (and so on) until I've worked my way down to one. Sometimes I pull five or six cards in a straight line, sometimes I make a circle or an X. These are outlined in the chapter on spreads. (See page 172)

Take a moment before you begin speaking and look carefully at the cards. It's at this moment a lot of Querents will ask if the cards are "ok" or if they're in some kind of trouble. Assure them that a pause on your part isn't a cause for alarm; that you just need to look at them for a moment and see what the common threads are.

Count the number of Swords, Coins, Cups, Wands and Major Arcana you find in the spread. This will determine what the theme (or themes) of the message is.

Swords can refer to stress, conflict, sexual issues, rumour, gossip, mental clarity.

Coins can refer to health and/or monetary issues.

Cups can refer to emotional issues and relationships.

Wands can refer to intellectual issues with a work or educational focus and energy.

A significant number of Major Arcana cards can indicate important life changes/challenges.

It may be helpful at this point to tell the Querent that you see a common thread or theme running throughout the spread. For example, if you see a lot of Coins you can explain that there seems to be a lot of emphasis on matters of health or money and ask if this is relevant to them. Remember, this is a dialogue, not a monologue. Ask for input and you will find the reading goes far smoother and is a more satisfying experience for both of you.

<u>Aces</u>

Energy

Prosperity

Quest

difficulty

disappointment

apathy

delay

Clarity

MINOR ARCANA

The Minor Arcana is made up of four suits. (Cups, Wands, Swords and Coins) The Minor Arcana generally tends to deal with the events of daily life: personal characteristics, emotional states, plans and desires for the future, energy, conflict and stress.

ACES

Aces are generally considered to be the root, the pure form of energy of each differing suit.

They can be interpreted as new beginnings, new projects, and new desires. They talk about the potential, not necessarily the outcome, of a situation. If a situation starts off badly perhaps it can be rescued but that may take a lot of effort and work. If a situation starts off well, it might not end well. All that the Ace can tell you is the potential, the raw material you've got to work with. When an Ace appears reversed, it can indicate an upheaval or a delay of some kind. It can also indicate that the "potential" inherent in each Ace is somehow lessened or possibly negated entirely.

The Ace of Cups
The Ace of Cups is about new beginnings in an emotional sense. There are those who connect the Ace of Cups with the Holy Grail, and as Grail lore was widely spread by the time the first tarot decks were being commissioned, this could be possible. However, it isn't a very current interpretation and not likely to come into a reading unless your Querent is literally on a

quest of some kind, in which case, it is likely that their quest has the potential to be successful, but again, one must look at the cards surrounding the Ace. If the Ace of Cups is Dignified it can signify love, abundance, a flow of energy. Note that it's not necessarily romantic love; it can indicate happiness and contentment, family relationships, spiritual health and awakening, peace, and forgiveness. It can also indicate the birth of a child in some cases.

Next to the Lovers, the Two of Cups, the Empress, the Ace of Cups can indicate the start of a lasting and successful relationship. Next to the Ten of Cups, it indicates reaching the desired outcome.

Ill Dignified: this can indicate problems. It can mean things got off to a bad start, that they're falling apart or simply that they'll be a bit delayed. It can mean that the love the Querent was hoping for might not last, or might not be as rewarding as they had hoped it would be. It can indicate things are likely to fall apart completely. It can indicate hurt and pain or some kind of chaos or emotional drain. The important thing to remember is that the cards next to it will help more fully explain what the Ace of Cups actually means.

The Ace of Cups ID next to the Six of Cups ID can speak of a relationship long since over which the Querent can not let go of. Next to the Nine of Swords, the failure of a relationship is causing anxiety and depression. Next to the Seven of Coins, the lack of success in a relationship can be directly connected to a lack of effort on the part of the participants.

The Ace of Swords

Like all Swords, the Ace is double-edged. In short, you can't make an omelette without breaking a few eggs, and when you've got a project or desire, other things often have to be sacrificed to get what you want. Dignified, the Ace of Swords is about energy, it's often connected to change. Imagine a big wind comes through your mind, clears out the cobwebs and gives you mental clarity. Did you ever just look at someone you loved through new eyes as if it was the first time you'd ever seen them? That's the effect of the Ace of Swords. It shows up in a spread usually at a time when the Querent is ready and strong enough to start making some changes in their life and at the moment when they look at their situation, maybe for the first time and think that something has to change.

The Ace of Swords next to the Devil indicates that an unhealthy relationship will reach a head. Next to the Moon, a lack of action on the part of the Querent results in disappointment and disillusionment. Next to the Chariot, the Querent will not meet her goals until she takes action.

III **Dignified:** just because you've got the sword, it doesn't make you right, or pure in intention. This can be one of those times when change is made at the hands of a person who's just cutting a swath through their friends, or being deliberately hurtful. Think about those times when someone decided they were going to change their life and they suddenly started becoming hurtful and nasty to those around them. Change can be happening a little too fast, and not in a good way. It can indicate a loss of hope, apathy or a refusal to defend yourself. It can simply mean a delay in the change, but it can also indicate a total abandonment of plan or a lack of desire to take care of yourself. Again, it depends on which cards it is surrounded by.

The Ace of Swords ID next to the Knight of Wands ID indicates that apathy has set in and must be dealt with. Next to the Nine of Wands, a sense of being over-burdened has left the Querent in a state of discomfort. Delegate, if possible. Next to the Seven of Swords ID, the Querent should take a closer look at who she surrounds herself by.

The Ace of Wands

Wands are generally considered to be energy, creativity, power. It is the spark that leads you someplace new, a new interest. Anything at all from religion, spirituality, vegetarianism, mechanics - anything is possible. It is creative energy. The Ace of Wands is a desire to try something new, to learn about something, to try something. It is embarking on a study programme or taking up yoga. In the Rider deck, the Ace of Wands looks like a torch, and it's this torch that lights the way. It doesn't tell you where to go, it just gives you the spark of interest that tells you it's a good time to try something new or learn something. It doesn't have the cutting capability of the Ace of Swords, but it's still strong.

The Ace of Wands next to the Fool indicates the beginning of a journey. Next to the Three of Coins, a new project will be helped along by careful, expert work. When the Ace of Wands appears next to the Tower ID, what was previously thought of as a disaster can be salvaged and is perhaps a blessing in disguise.

III Dignified: it can indicate a sense of disappointment, a lack of interest, apathy, boredom, a sense of failure, a project that seemed promising has fallen through, a promised job didn't materialise, your new guru turned out to be a dud. It can also indicate a delay, the changes you wanted to make will be made, just not right now. This can lead to frustration, there needs to be an element of patience exercised. It can indicate some kind of block, mental or physical, which can only be undone in time and with peace and calm.

The Ace of Wands ID next to the Four of Swords ID can speak of extreme apathy. Next to the Two of Wands, a new direction may help the Querent regain their enthusiasm. Next to the Eight of Coins, the Querent must keep in mind that their future rewards will be directly related to the efforts they make now.

The Ace of Coins
Coins, also called Pentacles, are largely about the material world, about money, health and concrete objects, but they can also be about a state of mind. Coins don't have the element of conflict or drama like Swords, or deal with emotional issues like Cups. They speak more about slow growth, about a need for things to be slow and steady in order to build a good foundation. Think of Coins as representing gracious individuals, people from families with old money who live with dignity. They can represent a gracious and elegant life-style, free from financial worry.

The Ace of Coins can indicate an unexpected inheritance, or a bit of money falling into your lap when you least expect it. The Ace of Coins is a powerful card; it's about lasting change for the better, a windfall, relief from financial difficulties, a new way of looking at prosperity. Good and lasting health.

When the Ace of Coins appears next to the Nine or Ten of Coins, it can indicate that if the Querent continues on the road they are on now and they continue to work hard, they will reap the rewards in the future. Next to the King of Coins ID, beware a person who promises a great deal and doesn't seem to be able to deliver. Next to the Emperor, be judicious in your dealings.

III Dignified: it can indicate problems. It can be merely a delay in plans, a new job, or financial relief, or it can indicate a serious problem with money, particularly the Querent's own way of looking at money, which could be desperate and grasping; they may have a belief that they're never going to have enough and so, in turn, that's what they get - never enough. It can indicate some kind of health problem which could become serious if not taken care of.

The Ace of Coins ID next to the Knight of Swords ID or the Moon ID can indicate dishonesty or fraud. The Querent must pay attention. Next to Temperance ID, the Querent is reminded that extreme behaviour will not help them achieve their goals.

Twos

Attraction

Imagination

Imbalance

deceit

Equilibrium

decisions

Trickery

Greed

Twos

The Two of Cups

This is a very positive card when it's upright. It can indicate an attraction, the start of a romance, the love for someone else that's finally been acknowledged. It can be an agreement, making up after a fight or a disagreement, calling a truce. It can be some form of cooperation or collaboration. It can indicate trust. Note that this doesn't have to refer only to romantic love, although that's how it's most often read. It can be family relationships, friendships, any place where two people come to an understanding, whatever that may be. It is important to be aware of the fact that when it comes to love, there is the need for both people to be mentally and spiritually healthy. For a relationship to succeed, both people must be balanced and equal. It is also important that their union isn't going to create disharmony somewhere else. (For example, two people cheating on their spouses might indeed be in love, but by virtue of how their relationship begins they are creating disharmony. Whether they are able to take that situation and channel it into a loving and open relationship depends largely on them.) Watch the cards surrounding the Two of Cups for clues as to how much balance and equality are present.

Indicators of good news laid next to the Two of Cups would be, for example, the Queen of Cups, Four of Wands, Ten of Cups, the Lovers or the Three of Coins.

Ill Dignified: the Two of Cups can be less lovely to see. It can indicate that an agreement or relationship is coming to an end, that there is deceit or vital information is being withheld. It could indicate that someone is cheating or that they want out of the relationship, that they have fallen out of love, or that they don't care to continue this friendship. Balance is off-kilter and disharmonious notes have been struck. It may not be beyond repair, but it's important to acknowledge that there is some discord.

Again, watch the cards around the Two of Cups ID. If you see, for example, the Five or the Seven of Swords, it may indicate things are not going well at all. The same can be said of the Three of Swords, the Ten of Swords, and the Five of Cups. These can indicate that things are simply not working out and that trying to force a relationship to work is as useless as trying to force liquid to stay in an upturned cup. What's going to happen is going to happen and no matter what you do or how you perform, it isn't going to make someone stay who doesn't want to be there.

The Two of Wands

If the Ace of Wands is the spark of imagination and the desire to change and to move ahead, the Two of Wands is the determination that gets you there. Think of this card as a compass that guides you, points in the correct direction and says GO! Most times, when people get this card (especially if the Four of Swords appears with it) they already know what it is they want to do, they just need to put their plan into action. This card is about power and about making things happen. It can also indicate success, vision, the power to sway others and get them to help you out and business acumen. It is the desire to succeed.

41

If you see this card next to the Magician, it's about the use of personal power and the discipline needed to succeed at something. It's reinforced when it's next to the Three of Coins, the World, Strength and the Chariot, as these are cards of movement. The Querent has the desire and the ability, and needs to begin to put these plans into action.

III Dignified: the Two of Wands ID can be about greed and ambition, the kind where people will step on you to get their way, and they are unaware (or uncaring) of hurting other people who they perceive as standing in their path. This would be a person who has a disproportionately large sense of entitlement *(I want what I want because I deserve it, and I get it because I want it, and if it hurts you, too bad)*. It can also indicate a loss of ambition or a loss of faith in yourself. Apathy can be indicated here. It can also be a warning to be careful of entering into a partnership where one person holds more power than the other as this can be destructive and detrimental.

Watch this card when you find it next to the Devil, the Queen of Cups ID, the Seven of Coins, the World ID, it serves to remind us that there is a lack of balance and respect.

The Two of Swords
This card can be read as a decision that has to be made. It is a choice between two more or less equal things. The Querent needs to weigh and balance the options carefully and pick the best one but s/he must also keep in mind that there may be little difference between the better choice and the worse. This card can also be about creating a delicate

balance in a difficult situation, about being diplomatic and careful at a time when diplomacy is difficult to maintain. It can mean not knowing what to do and so choosing to do nothing. Be aware, however, that doing nothing can bring about consequences that do not make you happy. When you choose not to act, someone else might choose for you and it might not be to your benefit.

The Two of Swords next to the Lovers indicates that a choice needs to be made, and that this choice will have a serious effect on a relationship. Next to the Empress ID, there is a sense that the Querent has lost their sense of proportion and needs to regain their footing. The Empress next to the Two of Swords ID can indicate that the Querent already knows which choice to make, they need only reflect on it.

III Dignified: this time, non-action is likely going to result in something negative. A choice needs to be made. It could be deceit, trickery, bad advice being deliberately given. It is a refusal to see things as they are, wilful blindness, continuing in a situation that has outlived its usefulness ages ago but not being willing to change, barriers between people, especially lovers, secrets being kept.

Watch this card when it appears next to the Empress ID, or the Seven of Swords. It indicates a lack of balance. Next to the Magician, it emphasises the need for diplomacy and careful action.

The Two of Coins
This card is about balance, about finding a way to maintain all your projects (work, home, study, love,

finances) and still have some fun. There's a delicate balance that all of us maintain and in the busy modern world, it wouldn't take much to upset that balance and make things complicated. It can appear when the Querent has been leading a life that lacks equilibrium as a reminder that they should either relax and enjoy themselves, or get to work and take up their responsibilities.

If it appears next to the Four of Wands, it's time to have some fun, to cut loose and relax. If it appears next to Temperance, it could indicate there's been too much cutting loose and relaxing going on, and that it's time to rein it in and get hold of yourself before your behaviour becomes problematic.

III Dignified: Here we have the classic lack of balance, a descent into addiction or the developing of bad habits you're going to have to pay for later on. It's simply being out of control. Overeating, overspending, overindulging, paying no attention to the warnings of friends and family, thinking you're invincible. This card reminds us that for every action, there's an equal and opposite reaction, and that the need to maintain a sense of equilibrium is very important. Eat too much, you feel sick or get fat. Eat too little and you hurt your body. Spend too much and you end up in trouble, spend too little and you deny yourself the good things in life.

The Two of Coins ID next to the Seven of Coins ID indicates that extreme behaviour or lack of balance will yield disappointing results. Next to the Moon, there is disillusionment. The Two of Coins ID next to the Tower can indicate that if the Querent doesn't buckle down and get serious, there could be unfortunate consequences.

<u>Threes</u>

Celebration

misled

depression

Strength

laziness

sorrow

diligence

Lack

The Three of Cups

This is a very positive card and one I always like to see in a reading. This card speaks of celebration, exuberance, joy. It can indicate the birth of a child, a marriage, or simply a party. It's about laughter, enjoyment, love. It's about friendship, support, and a sense of happiness. There is the indication here that something will occur which will be happily welcomed. The Three of Cups indicates a joyful celebration – but remember that joy is fleeting. Happiness and contentment are a different matter.

If it appears next to a less positive card such as the Three of Swords, it could potentially help to mitigate the negative effect of that card somewhat. There will be sorrow but even when there's sorrow you'll be able to find some joy or something to celebrate. Next to the Empress or the Page of Cups it can indicate the birth of a child or a creative project of some kind. Next to the Tower, it can indicate that what was previously thought of as a disaster will either be averted or in some way prove to be to the Querent's benefit.

III Dignified: The Three of Cups indicates the end of the party. Things could come apart, what was a good time may degenerate into a bad deal. Sex without love, promiscuity, a lack of self respect. Being taken advantage of by someone who you thought loved you and had your best interests at heart. There is a lack of money, love, respect, self respect, honesty, transparency or even decency. Like most reversed cards, it can indicate that there's going to be a delay or the effect of the card will be muted, as opposed to the joyous celebration the Querent was hoping for.

If you see the Ten of Swords, for example, next to the Three of Cups ID, it indicates some serious issues. There is the potential that the Querent has been or is going to be hurt and betrayed by someone, or even that the Querent is betrayer. If this is an action which is going to happen to the Querent, it's going to be unexpected and it's likely going to leave a mark. If you see the Three of Cups ID next to the Ten of Cups (joy, fulfilment), it just means the celebration might be a bit delayed, but rest easy, it's coming all the same. Next to the Tower, carelessness has led to calamity.

The Three of Wands

The Three of Wands is about putting a plan into action and having the strength to do the things that need to be done. It can be about partnership or cooperation, careful planning, strategy. It's about the courage and intelligence needed to make your way into a new project or to start something new. Established strength, success after an initial hardship, plans and ventures moving ahead. Think of this as the card that symbolises the desire to get out of a bad situation and making your way forward. It takes courage and a presence of mind to change your circumstances.

The Three of Wands next to the Ace of Swords indicates energy, a plan, getting things done. It's a sign of success or finally reaching your goals. If you find the Three of Wands next to the Two of Cups, this is also positive. Imagine it's a couple who have a plan to build a house or take a trip together. It indicates that their relationship will lend itself to meaningful projects. Next to the Eight of Coins, it indicates that diligent work will be rewarded appropriately.

III Dignified: This card can indicate the presence of someone who talks a good deal but has little to back up their words. There could also be the notion of being misled, possibly deliberately by someone who is eager to appear more in control or more successful than they really are. It can be about plans that have failed or are failing because someone isn't pulling their weight. It can be a loss of direction. The Querent just can't seem to find his way home. There is a lack of realism, a bad plan, or no plan at all. Complete inertia.

If you see the Three of Wands ID next to the Ace of Swords ID, it can indicate disharmony, a project or a plan heading for disaster. The Three of Wands ID next to the Seven of Swords could indicate that someone is leading the Querent up the garden path (or the Querent is doing the leading), and maybe even deliberately wasting their time and abusing their trust. Next to Justice, an individual who has been lazy or untruthful in their work will be exposed.

The Three of Swords
This is the most sorrowful card in the deck. It speaks of loss, betrayal, separation, heartache of the greatest kind. It's a loss you feel very, very deeply. What once was together will come apart. This card comes up when the Querent is at the tail-end of a relationship. When surrounded by mitigating cards it can indicate a bump in the road, a difficult patch in a relationship, a feeling of separation. The Querent must take care that these

feelings of sorrow don't deepen and descend into actual clinical depression.

If you see the Three of Swords with the Two of Cups, ID or the Lovers, it could be a sign that things in a relationship are going badly or are about to. Next to the Four of Cups ID, jealousy and possessiveness have caused a rift in a relationship that may be irreparable. Next to the Moon, the Querent's feelings of sadness are pulling them down into a depression. It is advisable for them to seek help.

III Dignified: it can mitigate the card or make it worse to have it reversed. It can indicate that things are so bad that there are thoughts of ending one's life. It can indicate a crippling depression, an almost manic sorrow that won't diminish. It can also indicate that though this hurts at the moment, it won't last forever. It's important to relay to the Querent that there is "another day" in the sense that though they might be feeling sad now and that this is a hard time, there will be better times ahead after this bad patch.

If you see the Three of Swords ID next to the Nine of Swords, sorrow and grief over a lost relationship is spilling over and the Querent may be starting to suffer physically. Next to the Queen of Swords ID, it is possible that the situation the Querent now finds herself in was orchestrated by someone intent on being hurtful. Next to the Knight of Cups, a loyal friend will help you through this crisis.

The Three of Coins
The Three of Coins is a card that speaks about the master craftsman. He's organised, diligent, honest,

he shows up for work on time, does his best, works with pride, works well with others, shares information, and creates something beautiful. This card is about the pride that we should take in our work, no matter how humble and that the rewards of hard work are satisfaction and pride in oneself. It's about knowing what needs to be done and then doing it properly.

If you see the Three of Coins next to the Magician, it indicates a real desire to work hard and to perfect a craft. There's a sense of diligence and honour about the work. If you see it next to the World it can be that this work will bring about a great deal of satisfaction as well as material rewards and recognition and the achievement of goals. Next to a more emotional card like the Lovers, it will indicate a commitment on the part of the Querent (or someone in the Querent's life) to work at their relationship, carefully building the foundations of a solid life together.

III Dignified: laziness, lost opportunities, not being fit to do a particular job, a lack of respect for the process, bad co-workers, disappointment with the results of work done, working in a careless, sloppy or haphazard way. People claiming they have abilities they do not have and when put to the test, their lies are exposed.

If the Three of Coins ID appears next to the Three of Wands, you've got the beginnings of a project going badly or already gone. If this card appears ID next to Justice or the Emperor, the Querent's (or someone else's) lack of regard for their work is going to catch up with them and they'll be called to account for their behaviour or their poor output. Next

51

to the Nine of Coins ID, the Querent may suffer some financial setback due to poor work habits.

<u>Fours</u>

consequences

vigour

Enjoyment

boredom

Jealousy

apathy

Greed

delay

The Four of Cups

Symbolises the boredom and apathy you get from having everything you want. The Querent is loved by his family, friends, his wife, and yet he still feels like something is missing. This isn't a card about seeking a spiritual "more" to your life, it's more about when people become self-absorbed and stop seeing the gifts they have in front of them. The idea that there's got to be something better out there can sometimes be followed by a sense of entitlement. How many times have you seen people who are dissatisfied with their lot and who decide they want something else and stop seeing what they do have? The result can be a selfish person who doesn't care who he hurts or who he steps on to get his desire. This card also appears to remind us of the things we do have; we are loved, we have friends, and at the very moment when we start taking those things for granted, we're in danger of losing them completely. It warns against complacency, against feeling no need for stimulation and growth within a relationship. There's always room for improvement, and there's always the possibility someone will leave or go away if you push them or if you simply stop caring about them and their feelings.

If you see the Four of Cups next to the Ace of Cups, you can imagine this person is stuck and stagnant, but that the seed of an idea has popped into their heads. It's time to clear the cobwebs and get a fresh perspective. The Four of Cups next to the Magician would remind us that it's time to exercise a little discipline and to really take stock of what we have in our arsenal. The Four of Cups next to the

Five of Coins is a shove in the right direction. You have so much more than you realise.

III Dignified: the Four of Cups can mean a renewed vigour for life; a fresh start; renewed energies. It can also be an enhanced sense of selfishness. It can be a gaping hole in someone's upbringing that causes them to think they're entitled to do and say and take whatever they please. This card appears when someone is undergoing some kind of crisis and they are getting carried away with their selfishness. They want what they want, and if it hurts you to get it, it's of little consequence to them. The Four of Cups ID can also be a reminder that it's time to stop a certain way of thinking before it becomes a problem, not after. It's harder to make up for things already done than to change the behaviours that could cause the problems. It's time to stop feeling sorry for ourselves and pick up our socks, get on with our lives and to respect the people around us.

If you see the Four of Cups ID next to the Empress/Emperor ID, you're dealing with an emotionally powerful person who insists on having their way. Next to the Page of Swords, this individual is bored and vindictive: a bad combination. Next to Temperance: self absorption had led to a dangerous lack of balance.

The Four of Swords
The Querent knows what he's meant to be doing. He knows if he's supposed to be studying, or getting a new job, or walking away from a bad relationship but he just isn't doing it and he's wasting his time and that of others. Sometimes the Querent is afraid of taking a risk; sometimes they fear the

consequences of their decisions; sometimes they're simply lazy. There's a sense of stagnation here and that can be a dangerous thing. While the Four of Swords ID can be read as stagnation and immobility, it can also be read as a time of rest and recovery after battle. It's important to take a time of peace or relaxation to recover, especially if you've been through a hard time. But pay attention: a truce does not equal peace. The time you have for recovery could be short, and you could find yourself back in hot water again so use the time for rest accordingly. It can be a time period after grief or loss, a readjustment to a new life. It could indicate a retreat; a hospitalisation for some illness; a necessary time of recovery.

The Four of Swords, next to the Three of Swords tells a story: A time of rest after a bad shock or a deep sadness. The Four of Swords next to the Two of Cups, ID indicates the party is over, you have to take some time to lick your wounds and then get yourself back together. Next to the Chariot ID, the Querent is apathetic and stagnant.

III Dignified: it can be either an extreme apathy or depression; an inability to get oneself moving. It can also be the end of that period and it was time to apply yourself and do what it is you know you're supposed to be doing. It could indicate depression; apathy; a need for recovery; a warning that too much stress can affect your health in adverse ways.

The Four of Swords ID next to the Tower is a sign that things have gone (or are going to go) completely wrong and that those things are going to significantly affect the Querent. Next to the Four of Cups it could indicate a person is just unwilling or unable to do the things they need to do to get on with their lives and find their way. Next to the Knight of Wands ID, a formerly energetic person has fallen into an apathetic state.

The Four of Wands

This is about celebration: some kind of exuberance; a party; a wedding; a holiday. It can indicate a well earned rest; laughter; a good time with friends; letting loose; enjoying oneself. The way that this card differs from the Two of Coins is that here there is the idea that once the party is over, it's time to get back to work and keep moving forwards. It can indicate taking part in a ceremony or some kind of rite; breaking the bonds that held you; a feeling of exhilaration; a sudden freedom. Now that one goal has been achieved, it's time to set another one and move forward. Don't get too hung up on past glories, it's time to make some new goals and then meet them.

Next to the Two of Cups it could indicate a wedding or a romance. Next to the Ace of Cups, it could indicate the start of a new relationship. Next to the Three of Coins, it could talk about the successful completion of a project and the feeling of elation that follows.

III Dignified: this card can indicate that the party is over and it's time to go home. It can come up when someone has been overindulging or has been touting themselves as fabulous without having the goods to back it up. It can indicate a delay of some kind, that the celebration is coming, but that it's going to be delayed in some fashion or not as a shiny and wonderful as the Querent had first imagined. A party falling flat: disappointment.

lll Dignified and next to the Lovers it could indicate trouble: A relationship long since gone sour that people persist in keeping alive. If it appears next to the Three of Swords, it gives the idea of some party or reason for celebrating that turns out to have some negative consequences. Next to the Two of Coins ID, balance has been lost. It's time for the Querent to get their feet back on the ground.

The Four of Coins

This card can be read as greed; possessiveness; lust. There's a sense here that Querent is simply hanging on too tightly to everything they have and that includes other people. It can indicate penny pinchers who can't bring themselves to have a good time because they're always calculating how much things are going to cost them. It can indicate that there's a need for care in financial matters. This card can oscillate a bit; it can be either be careful with your money or don't be so careful with your money.

If you see this card next to the Seven of Swords, there is the sense of being used or being conned. If you see it next to the Lovers it can indicate a relationship in tatters due to jealousy and possessiveness. If you see the Four of Coins next to the Three of Swords, the Querent (or someone close to him) is extremely jealous, and their lack of reason is about to cause the loss of their primary relationship or to cause sorrow and grief.

III Dignified: this is jealousy gone horribly wrong. This is a possessiveness that chokes other people completely. An inability to take into consideration the feelings of others; it is a greed and all consuming need to have everything all for yourself. This is being conned or being used by someone. Stupid business deals inexpertly done and foolishly executed. A massive financial setback, ridiculous and intemperate spending that leads to problems.

Next to the Nine of Coins also ID. it would indicate a financial fall. Imagine this card next the Lovers, it would be a relationship so incredibly discordant it could only be described as toxic. If this card is next to the Death card it could indicate that someone's jealousy is going to get so out of hand that it's going to completely destroy their relationship and possibly cause harm to someone.

Fives

Hope

Sabotage

Abuse

Competition

self-pity

Unkindness

Hardship

Poverty

FIVES

The Five of Cups

The Five of Cups can remind us that we're down but not out and that although the Querent may have suffered some losses they haven't fallen under completely. It can remind us of the importance of hanging on to the good we have and letting go of the bad. It can be a warning that a loss is about to happen, that there's trouble brewing on the horizon, and that if the Querent isn't careful (or even if they are) things can fall apart. The Five of Cups reminds us not to hang on to the loss and to hang on instead to what remains. To let go of things that hold us down. This can also indicate unfair treatment at the hands of someone else, an unhappy marriage, a feeling of isolation. This card reminds us that the biggest mistake we can make is feeling sorry for ourselves and letting ourselves feel that we're victims.

If you see the Five of Cups next to the Two of Cups ID it could indicate relationship troubles heading in the Querent's direction. If you see the Five of Cups with the Ace of Swords ID it could indicate some kind of abusive relationship the Querent is involved in. Next to the Eight of Wands, a message is coming, one that could alleviate the Querent's suffering.

III Dignified: the Five of Cups can talk about a person who has spiralled into self pity that seems endless and that they're in fact alienating themselves from loved ones and friends because of their constant focus on their losses. It can indicate an imbalance of emotion, a desire to see themselves as the victim of something unfair; a selfishness. It can talk about a relationship that has gone off the rails and is so completely unhealthy that there's no hope left. It can alternately mean that an old friend or lover will contact the Querent. It can indicate an unexpected gift, some kind of hope, a personal fulfilment.

The Five of Cups ID next to the Three of Swords talks about a serious depression or the potential of experiencing serious upheaval and loss. Next to the Ace of Cups ID, a love relationship is experiencing a difficult time. Next to the Six of Coins, take the help that is offered.

The Five of Wands

This speaks about competition and about not being afraid to put yourself into the middle of the fray. If you're competing with your fellow students or co-workers or family members, don't be shy – do your best and participate but remember never to lose your self-respect or step on someone to achieve your goals. This is a card about healthy competition, about putting your name forward and demanding recognition for what you've done, but not in an aggressive fashion. Remember the difference between assertiveness and aggression. Too many times people don't get what it is that they want because they simply don't ask for it. The Five of Wands says it's time to get in on the action, not time to be timid and modest. It can also be the onset of conflict, interpersonal problems; crisis.

If you see the Five of Wands next to the Two of Swords it could mean that it's time to put yourself forward at work, to ask for a promotion or to accept new responsibilities. If you get the Five of Wands next to the Three of Coins it could indicate that the Querent's participation in some kind of competition or a display of their talents could result in new respect and rewards at work. Next to the Four of Swords, apathy is ruining the Querent's chances. His lack of energy is being noticed by others.

III Dignified: the Five of Wands can talk about an unhealthy competition, one that has got completely out of hand as in one between siblings who compete for their parents' affection or co-workers who take credit for your work or try to sabotage your efforts. It can speak of someone who is envious and in fact they are letting their envy get in the way of their better judgement. It can talk about being taken in by a con artist or a sophisticated liar and the need to recognise the truth and deal with it head on.

Five of Wands, ID next to the Ace of Swords could indicate a new project that's going to require co-operation or better yet, inspire the co-operation of others; that people could be coming together for a common good. The Five of Wands ID next to the Queen of Swords ID, could indicate a serious interpersonal issue and it could get out of hand. Next to the Four of Coins ID, a spiteful and jealous person has been making problems for the Querent. Tread carefully.

The Five of Swords
Is a card that indicates that someone has been deliberately unkind. They've intentionally hurt another person with their words or their actions. They've spread rumours, or humiliated someone knowing exactly what the effect of their word was going to be. It wasn't an accident and can't be

explained away nicely. Often this unkindness was unexpected and shocking on the part of the recipient. This card comes up as a warning: prepare yourself, gird your loins because there's some nastiness afoot. It can also come up after the fact. There could be some kind of acknowledgement that someone has been rude.

If you see the Five of Swords next to the Three of Swords, the situation has gotten or is about to get out of hand and cause a rift. The Querent is likely to suffer for it, grieving the loss of a friend or partner. The Five of Swords next to any Queen (especially if the Queen is ID) means that the harsh words have likely come from a woman, older and sometimes a person in authority like a boss or a relative. Next to the Nine of Swords, this conflict has caused great anxiety. Healing is needed.

III Dignified: the Five of Swords can speak of an abusive situation getting out of hand. Someone is operating under the erroneous belief that they can do or say whatever they please and that the people around them exist solely for their purposes. If the Querent is the victim of this person, they need to re-evaluate their relationship and decide how much they really need to be around someone who is hurling abuse at them. Sometimes these things happen so gradually that we don't even realise what's going on but when a card like this comes up, it's sent to remind us that abuse in any form is unacceptable and we need to take a step back, either from our behaviour or the behaviour of others.

The Five of Swords ID next to the Ten of Swords, it can indicate that a person has taken a dislike to another and is actively seeking to make trouble for them. Next to the Four of Cups, it could be some harsh words that have marred a friendship. Next to the Tower, things will come to a head, abusive words or harmful gossip will be exposed.

The Five of Coins

This speaks about hardship, certainly, but it is also about biting off your nose to spite your face. The Querent (or someone close to them) has refused offers of help, has walked a path that they knew was going to hurt them, has participated in activities that were destructive or detrimental. Why will they not accept help when it's offered or take a less destructive path? Maybe their beliefs hold them back; maybe they're too stubborn; maybe they were not willing to compromise in the past. The point is that they've got no one to blame but themselves. More flexibility would be helpful, a willingness to bend, a willingness to unclench your fist and take help when offered. It can also be loneliness; isolation; separation; spiritual problems; poor health.

Five of Coins next to the card for Temperance indicates that the Querent (or someone close to them) has some kind of addiction problem and that it could be more serious than first thought. It could get to the point where money starts to become a problem or perhaps it already has become a problem. If you get the Five of Coins next to the Ace of Coins, it could indicate that hard times are a thing of the past.

III Dignified: the Five of Coins can mean either wretched poverty or serious economic hardship. This may or may not be the fault of the Querent, (gambling on the part of a partner; a loss in the financial markets; it could be anything) It could also be a release from poverty, an unexpected gift that eases their discomfort, sudden wealth.

Next to the Ace of Coins ID, this card could mean that hard times have only just begun or they will get worse before they get better. Next to the Six of Swords ID, suffering will be eased. Next to the Six of Coins, someone will offer to help the Querent and provided there are no strings attached, the Querent should swallow their pride and accept.

<u>Sixes</u>

Nostalgia

Peace

mourning

Charity

Victory

defeat

Trouble

Stingy

The Six of Cups

This is a card that talks about old relationships and old friendships. It can speak of gestures of affection, sex, seeing the world through the open and accepting eyes of a child. It's a card rooted in nostalgia and happy memories. Often this card indicates that the Querent is going to hear from a long lost friend, or an old lover. It can talk about how we romanticise the past, how old times always look a little rosier than where we are now. We remember past romances as being better than they actually were. It can indicate that the Querent is focussing on the past at the expense of the present.

If you see the Six of Cups next to the Lovers, it could indicate that the Querent has been directing a lot of energy thinking about an old relationship, or that this person will be contacting the Querent or running into him accidentally somewhere. If the Six of Cups comes next to the Three of Swords, it could indicate that the Querent's nostalgia is tinged with grief, that the thing they are hoping for is gone; that they need to see things in a more realistic light. Next to the Ten of Cups, it can indicate that a link with the past will bring peace and joy.

III Dignified: the danger is that the Querent is spending all her energy looking into the past and very little of it living in the moment. Past relationships and situations have become distorted and unrealistic. This could indicate an imbalance, a desire for a love relationship or a friend long gone. This is mourning without ceasing to the detriment of the present moment. This card comes up to remind us that living in the past will not create a future. A future is created by work done in the present. It can indicate an unwelcome contact with a person from the Querent's past. It can also indicate an old romance being reignited, but be warned, this relationship broke up for a reason and that what tore the relationship apart in the first place has likely not changed.

The Six of Cups, ID, next to the Queen of Cups, ID indicates things have gotten out of hand, that the Querent's desire for the past is becoming unhealthy, that it's impossible to move forward in life with eyes cast back. Next to the Eight of Wands, a message is coming from someone from the Querent's past. It may not entirely be of a welcome nature. Next to the Nine of Swords, longing for something long past is the cause of anxiety and sorrow.

The Six of Swords

In some decks, this card shows a boatman ferrying a woman and a child away from choppy waters and towards peace. This card often comes up when a problem has almost been dealt with, when a crisis is over (or nearly over) and the Querent needs reassuring that the worst is over and that there will be a time of retreat and regrouping. This card also comes up sometimes when the Querent has had some serious issues and it seems to them that the only way to deal with those problems is to leave and to go to another place. This card can indicate a feeling of being 'haunted' or followed by someone or something, and that closure is necessary.

If you find the Six of Swords next to the Three of Swords, or the Ten of Swords, or the Tower, there could be a serious upheaval in the life of the

Querent. If the Six of Swords appears next to the Star, especially ID, it could indicate a prolonged feeling of sadness or depression. There's a sense that a cloud is hanging over the Querent and that things are going downhill.

III Dignified: the Six of Swords can mean the trouble is just beginning, that once you put out one fire another one calls your attention. It can indicate that difficulty is just starting, but to hang on because there's an end in sight to all of this. It can also mean there's going to be some temporary relief, a tiny but much needed respite before heading back out into battle. Things are going to get worse before they get better, but they will get better, so take heart.

The Six of Swords ID next to the Seven of Swords may indicate that thievery or trickery could be at the heart of the Querent's current sorrow. Next to the King of Swords: look to an older/authoritative male figure for some relief or protection. Next to the Four of Swords (especially ID) a lack of action on someone's part is the cause of the current situation. Next to the Four of Cups ID, the indication is that there will be a temptation to put your problems aside by distracting yourself with other things. Be wary of letting those distractions get in the way of your life.

The Six of Wands

This is a card that speaks of victory. It can indicate a spiritual change or understanding, but it is most often read as a victory in the here and now. If the Five of Wands speaks of the need to participate in the competition, the Six of Wands speaks of the outcome. The Six of Wands is also about the use of diplomacy to solve a problem rather than brute force. The quick thinking and grace that accompanies this card are what gives it the sense of victory. When faced with a problem, the Querent found a solution and overcame that problem, but it is important to remember that the battle may be won, but the war might not be over, so the Querent needs to remember not to let pride in this victory turn to arrogance or complacency.

If you see the Six of Swords next to the Four of Cups, Two of Cups, the Lovers, the Three of Cups, there will be cause for celebration. Something the Querent has wanted for a while will come to fruition. If you get the Six of Swords next to Justice, a decision will go in the Querent's favour.

III Dignified: it can be victory delayed, or not quite as splendid as the Querent had hoped. Something has fallen flat. It can indicate bad and hurtful gossip, enemies lining up to do some damage, rumours designed to cause problems. It can mean delayed or bad news coming. It can mean a sense of paranoia on the part of the Querent; it can indicate arrogance, smugness or complacency that could lead to one's eventual downfall.

The Six of Swords ID next to the Ten of Swords or the Seven of Swords can indicate that there are other people out there who wish to cause problems for the Querent. Be careful not to give people who wish you harm any ammunition. Be very careful who you trust. Next to the World ID, the belief that victory is at hand or that the Querent will get what they want is about to be challenged. Things are not turning out the way the Querent had originally (and possibly arrogantly) thought they would.

The Six of Coins

This card speaks of charity, generosity and giving. It can mean giving money to someone in need, or it can indicate emotional or spiritual generosity. It can be about someone lending an ear or emotional support at a time when it is greatly needed. This card reminds us that giving to others creates a flow of energy which is beneficial and positive for everyone involved. It can indicate a relief from financial problems, possibly from an unexpected source. There could be a windfall, or a surprising piece of good luck. This card can also speak of debts being cleared away, kindness, sympathy.

If you see the Six of Coins next to the Ten of Cups, the wish fulfilment card, there could be a sense of relief. Financial burdens being lifted. The Six of Coins next to a King or a Queen indicate an older person who has achieved some success and is now sharing with others. The Six of Coins next to the Eight of Coins indicates a past investment or project could be the source of financial relief.

Ill Dignified: the Six of Coins can talk about the sort of charity that has strings attached. It's the sort of help that leave the Querent indebted to a person who is more than happy to remind them of that debt on a regular basis. It can speak about recklessness with money, crazy spending without looking ahead to the future. It can indicate someone who is being stingy and tight and causing others to suffer because of their attachment to money. If the Querent is being taken advantage of, it's time for them to put their foot down.

The Six of Coins ID next to the Five of Coins speaks of further financial hardships; lean times ahead; problems which will take a long time to solve. Next to the Queen of Coins ID, beware of accepting money or help from a person who is likely to lord it over you. Pay it back as soon as possible to get this person to stop berating you. Next to the Nine of Cups ID, if the Querent is thinking of asking for money or help from an individual who is wealthy but not generous, it would be better to look elsewhere. This person is not likely to be helpful out of the goodness of their heart.

Sevens

Trust

Illusion

Embattled

vindication

Inertia

Overwhelmed

Confusion

disappointment

The Seven of Cups

The Seven of Cups is a card that talks about illusion, about the difference between reality and what passes for reality. It's about too many choices and the fact that some of these choices look better than they are. This card can come up when the Querent finds herself stuck in some way, unable to make a decision about a course of action. It warns that some of these paths she might elect to take are not what they seem and that a careful decision must be made. This card can also be about a fantasy that gets out of hand, about plans that are being made that are "pie in the sky" and without a basis in reality. The Querent is dealing with confusion in their personal life, confusion that might be of their own making or it might be that someone else is clouding their judgment. Be careful of investments that promise huge returns in a short time; be careful of people who make offers of employment that seem too good to be true. This card speaks of people who will lie or omit the truth, who will make things seem better than they are.

Next to the Three of Wands ID, it indicates that someone is leading the Querent up the garden path, they are being deliberately deceived. Next to the Three of Swords, it can indicate some great sorrow or problems could be the result of indecision or a decision badly taken. Next to the Ace of Swords, it could indicate that sudden clarity will reveal the truth about something, helping the Querent while she makes a decision about her life.

III **Dignified:** this can be confusion that is completely out of hand, almost to the point of delusion. It can speak of the Querent as being completely blinded by dreams which have no basis in reality. It can also be truth revealed (possibly after a time of being lied to or having believed something that wasn't true) or a sense of knowing when someone is lying to you. It can be the ability to see through lies and to follow a definite path, to make concrete plans and to follow through. It can indicate a fear of success, an inability to follow through with plans, a desire to let someone else make a decision for you and to abdicate responsibility. Beware of the temptation to let someone else do your thinking for you; if later on you don't like the results, you've got no one to blame but yourself.

Next to the Page of Swords this could indicate that someone is spreading rumours or making problems. Next to the Three of Coins ID, deception could have a financial connection, there could be a con-artist at work. Next to the Lovers ID, love is blind to the point of doing harm. The Querent needs to open his eyes and see his relationship clearly.

The Seven of Swords
This card is about putting your trust in an untrustworthy place, investing emotionally or financially with someone whose main goal was to trick you or to take from you. This card can also indicate deliberate cruelty, often from an unexpected source. This is the kind of cruelty that takes your breath away, and leaves you thinking "what just happened?" This card can also be about a con man, a trickster, a scam. It can indicate that someone is trying to make gains by being deceitful at work or in their personal lives. But this card carries a warning - those who win by trickery will

76

eventually be exposed, and if the Querent is being dishonest they should know that this dishonesty is going to cost them in the end. It can indicate that there's a need for diplomacy and withholding information until the right moment. It can indicate that there may be a need for the kind of cunning that might normally be morally repugnant to you. Just remember that everything you do in this life counts and if you think the only way to win is to cheat, you have to decide how much you want to win, how worth it is really is to sacrifice your ethics and morals.

III Dignified: it can indicate an apology or a vindication of sorts. Someone has wronged the Querent, deliberately, maybe publicly, and the Querent was justifiably shocked and hurt by this action. Vindication is at hand, it could be someone acknowledging that what this person did was horrible. It could be an apology from the person who was hurtful. It could be the return of lost property, something that was taken from you will be returned to you. If the Querent is the one who did the taking, they'd better be very careful, because this card could mean exposure of their behaviour and a loss of face.

Next to the Four of Wands ID, the Six of Cups ID, the Lovers, the Emperor, the Empress etc., someone close to the Querent is being dishonest. Next to Justice, it would bring to mind the idea of vindication/justice. Next to the Fool, especially ID, you get the sense that someone is taking advantage of a person who is naive and trusting and that they may well get away with their crimes.

The Seven of Wands

This card is about being embattled, being under siege at the moment when you least need it (and do you ever need it?). Hold your ground, stand up for your beliefs, even if others think you wrong. It warns the Querent that being aggressive may have unintended consequences. If fighting is unavoidable and there does not seem any other way out, then the Querent must be prepared to do battle and to be aware that they may find themselves in over their heads. You could also read this card as being overwhelmed with work or other responsibilities. It might be a good time for the Querent to learn to say no once in a while, and to say "I've got other responsibilities" in order to avoid being burdened with things they can't or don't want to handle. The Querent must be aware of her limits and refuse to bite off more than she can chew.

Next to the Three of Coins, it could indicate that the current struggle (possibly work related) could result in more ability or satisfaction at work and that a project that seems overwhelming will work out well and give the Querent more credibility at work. If you find the Seven of Wands next to the Emperor ID or one of the court cards (especially ID), you may very well find that the Querent is engaged in some kind of battle with a person they know and that they want something from someone which is unreasonable or that perhaps this person isn't able to give.

III Dignified: it can indicate being overwhelmed to the point of being nearly ill or refusing to accept anymore responsibilities and walking away from problems. It could indicate a person who's so aggressive that they're practically out of control or it could indicate someone who is so passive they're being walked on and treated badly. It can indicate indecision, retreat, lost opportunities through inaction, giving up when going forward would have been advisable.

Next to the Four of Swords ID, apathy and a lack of motion have caused greater troubles than the Querent could have anticipated. Next to the High Priestess or the Queen of Swords, the Querent will need to gather their inner strength in order to manage a difficult time. Help from an older female could be in order.

The Seven of Coins

This card can be read as disappointment with what you've reaped. The Querent expected more and got less but that could be because they failed to put enough effort into something and were hoping to reap miraculous rewards. This card can be a bit of a "you've got nobody to blame but yourself card" which is a message not many people want to hear. This card does not speak about disaster but about a set-back or a result that wasn't as fabulous as had been hoped. It doesn't speak of ruin but then again the hoped for opportunity could be gone and it may not be possible to go back and do over whatever it was they should have done better the first time. This card can also be a reminder to have some patience, that the Querent can't control the outcome of everything and that sometimes they just have to sit and wait for a while and see what will happen.

If you see the Seven of Coins next to the Two of Coins (especially ID) the Querent has been having too much fun at the expense of things that they should have taken more seriously. If you see the

Seven of Swords next to one of the Aces, especially the Ace of Coins or Wands, you might get the idea that the project that initially sounded good and looked promising has turned out to be less than what was originally imagined but that might very well be the fault of the people involved. If you see the Ace of Coins next to the Seven of Swords, don't discount the idea that someone may have sabotaged the Querent's efforts or that they have been tricked in some way and that their disappointment is not entirely due to their own behaviour.

III Dignified: it can speak of a complete and total inertia leading to serious problems. Being 'frozen' by fear or apathy and the resulting problems that arise from inaction. It can indicate money problems or some kind of imbalance. Investments that don't do as well as hoped or which do poorly can be indicated here. It could be money problems of the self-induced kind or a warning about financial failure that could result in bankruptcy. It can speak of a situation being out of control, a money pit of some kind where the Querent finds himself throwing money away continually in the hopes of rescuing some project such as house renovations or car repairs which are going to be costly and cause a lot of trouble.

Next to the Eight of Wands ID, the Querent may discover news of an unpleasant nature relating to money. Next to the Star, what was hoped for will either be far less than originally imagined or not happen at all. Next to the Knight of Coins ID, losses could be greater than first thought.

Eights

Struggle

Freedom

rewards

delay

Trapped

Action

laziness

Out of Control

The Eight of Cups

The Eight of Cups is a card that speaks about having the savvy to know when to walk away from a situation. Something in the Querent's life is not working and it hasn't been working for a long time and they are getting to the point where they may feel fed up or exhausted. This card often comes up when the Querent is involved in a one sided relationship, a friendship that is all giving and no receiving, a job that is wearing her out and leaving her exhausted and drained.

This card can also come up when the Querent knows that their struggle is useless, that instead of making things better, things are getting worse or staying the same. There's a sense of weariness that comes with this card, that moment when you think that you're so fed up that you just can't take it anymore. This card can also indicate that a person who has been living in the past needs to get themselves together and go forward into the future. They need to leave behind the things that have been weighing them down in order to experience and enjoy what will come.

Next to the Three of Wands, it could indicate movement of some kind, a physical move, a new job, a new venture. If you see it next to Death, the Lovers, or the Two of Cups (especially ID), it could indicate a relationship that has lasted for as long as possible and is now over. It is an upheaval of some kind, a major change in the life of the Querent. If you see it next to the Tower, it could indicate the same kind of major shift but of a potentially catastrophic nature.

III Dignified: the Eight of Cups can be a breaking free of old habits, a move to a new place, starting a new life, similar to when the card is Dignified but in a more dramatic fashion. This would be for a big move, a big break, a radical change in lifestyle. Alternately, it can also indicate that the Querent is really hopelessly stuck in a pattern that's bad for them and making them miserable, that they are inert and in danger of getting sucked under.

Next to the Two of Swords, it can speak about a decision that needs to be made. Often people know what the right decision is already, that it's not so much about a dilemma of choice but panic or nerves about how to put that choice into action. Next to the Devil, the Querent feels trapped in an unhealthy relationship. They want to leave but are afraid. Next to the Eight of Wands, a new piece of information could help the Querent make up her mind.

The Eight of Swords

This is a card that speaks about difficult situations, feeling trapped, feeling that you can't move forward and you can't go backwards. This card often comes up when the Querent finds themselves in a rough situation and fears the consequences of moving on, speaking up, telling the truth, breaking up, letting go of an addiction, telling someone they don't want to continue a friendship/relationship with them, finding a new job, etc. The choice they have to make isn't easy and the Querent will likely have to suffer for their convictions or their needs but if they don't make this move, they will find themselves suffering even more and for longer. This card can also come up when people feel powerless and legitimately don't know what to do. It can come up for people who are trying to avoid responsibility for their actions. This is the card that comes up for the Querent who is always on the lookout for the White Knight who's going to rescue her and make her a whole person. This can speak of learned helplessness.

If you see the Eight of Swords next to the Eight of Cups, it can indicate that the situation has reached a peak and that the Querent is going to walk away. If you see it next to the Emperor or one of the court cards (ID) it can indicate a personal relationship that has gone sour and is trapped in an unhealthy cycle. Next to the Ace of Swords, it can indicate that sudden mental clarity is going to give the Querent the strength and presence of mind they need to make their move.

III Dignified: the Eight of Swords can be a situation that's so out of control that the Querent is likely to suffer some real damage. (Unless the Querent is causing the damage, or is watching a friend or loved one suffer) You could read it as an addiction out of control, a lifestyle that seems to offer no hope and no future, a marriage that's turned into a prison. It can also be read as a breaking free of the bonds that held them, a realisation that they are in control of their lives and a desire to make decisions that benefit them.

Next to the Moon (especially ID) there's a sense that the situation is becoming serious, that their feelings of being trapped are leading to depression and sadness. Next to the Nine of Swords, the Querent's situation is the cause of anxiety and worry. Next to the Nine of Swords, the Querent needs to remember that she is the only person holding her back from what she wants.

The Eight of Wands

This card can be read as one of action, energy. Making a decision, making a move, taking charge of your life and doing something about it. This card can indicate that a message is coming. The message that's on its way to the Querent is usually something of importance, a missing piece of information that could help them to make a decision or the truth about something. It's not your run-of-the-mill email or text message. This card speaks about information that illuminates a situation or gives the Querent the ammunition they need. It's not necessarily a message in the traditional sense of a letter or a phone call, it can also be a conversation where truth is revealed by a third party, a newspaper article, a conversation overheard, seeing someone do something that tells you the truth about them. Imagine that someone has been telling only half the story, and then by accident you discover something that tells you the other half. It can indicate that the Querent will be hearing from someone important or someone they haven't heard from in a while.

If you see the Eight of Wands next to the Lovers, the Six of Cups, or the Two of Cups, the message may be of a positive nature and will probably come from an old friend or an old lover. If you see the Eight of Wands next to the Ace of Cups, it could mean that an old relationship or friendship is about to be rekindled.

Ill Dignified: it could be a message delayed, a piece of information revealed after the fact. It could be bad news, or news that's been distorted somehow, so pay attention. It could be gossip; rumour or untrue bits of information being spread around by someone who's either ill informed or malicious.

Watch this card if you happen to see it next to the Page of Swords, especially if it's Ill Dignified as it can be malicious gossip or rumour. Next to the Eight of Wands there is the hint of gossip or someone talking out of turn. Someone has not been one hundred percent truthful and their lies will be revealed.

The Eight of Coins

If the Seven of Coins is about disappointment, the Eight speaks of the rewards of careful and diligent work. Imagine the Querent did very little and then was disappointed with the results of an exam. She felt that she could do better and then applied herself very carefully and worked very hard and on the next exam she scored a much higher mark. The Eight of Coins tells us that the rewards for our work are very real and that if we want to succeed, real work is going to be required. Even when it seems like the task is too difficult or too much trouble, this card reminds us to keep working and not to give up. It warns against giving up before the job is finished or not finishing what you've started. This card often comes up in relation to studies, that someone is thinking of quitting something and this card reminds them to keep going, the benefits of continuing outweigh the immediate relief of walking away. This card can also indicate a small gain in finances, nothing extravagant, but it could indicate a pay raise at work (as the result of good performance) or maybe a gift of some money.

If you see the Eight of Coins next to the Magician, you get the idea that Querent has a project about which there will be a great deal of learning involved and that this learning needs to be carefully organised, logical and the need to apply themselves will be great. The Eight of Coins next to the Five of Swords speaks of the need to compete in order to accomplish their goals or that there may be some obstacles, but to continue anyway. It warns the Querent to be wary of people who try to block their progress and to continue even if they're not fully supported by others. The Eight of Coins next to the Ace of Coins or the Ace of Wands/Swords speaks of a project that could potentially be quite important.

III Dignified: the Eight of Coins ID can talk about a dislike or distaste for hard work. It can indicate that the Querent is not using her talents to their fullest, that she's in danger of becoming apathetic. It could indicate that the end is further than she originally thought and that her project will be delayed, but that she should continue. It could indicate a level of dishonesty in business, so the Querent may need to be careful.

Next to the Five of Coins, remind the Querent that apathy or a lack of effort will not only be a disappointment but could have financial or emotional consequences. Next to the Fool ID, someone is shirking their responsibilities with potentially disastrous results. Next to the Knight of Coins ID, disorganisation and laziness will lead nowhere. The Querent must take charge and be responsible.

<u>Nines</u>

Satisfaction

decadence

depression

Smugness

Luxury

Failure

Anxiety

Health

The Nine of Cups

This card indicates satisfaction, good health and pleasure. It can be the solidification of a relationship, the pleasure of company, the achievement of a goal or dream. This is about all manner of satisfaction, sensual, physical, also spiritual. This card can be about obtaining what it is you think you want, but the warning implicit here is that what we think we want is rarely what we need at the end of the day. It can hint at a little smugness about success. Be careful of being too proud of what you've got, everything is impermanent and therefore can go away just as easily as it can come to you.

If you see the Nine of Cups next to the Ace of Cups, the Ace of Swords or the Ace of Coins, it could indicate that a new project or relationship will bear fruit and be successful. A blossoming of a relationship is indicated when the Nine of Cups appears next to the Lovers or the Two of Cups. Next to Temperance, it's a warning not to get too carried away.

Ill Dignified: this card can indicate smugness out of control, selfishness, a refusal to share and be generous with those around you. The Querent may also be in danger of hurting themselves through excess: drugs, drinking, spending, they are walking a fine line between enjoying life and hurting themselves. Something has spun out of control. Vanity can also be indicated here. This card can be about someone who has what it is you want, and you might have to dance to their tune to get it. This can lead to uncomfortable compromises and a feeling of having something held over your head.

If you see this card III Dignified next to the Three of Swords, the excesses in the life of the Querent (or someone close to them) are going to cause great sorrow. If you see it next to a court card, or next to the Emperor or Empress ID, the Querent is near someone who is behaving in this manner, and that their actions are affecting those around them.

The Nine of Swords
This card indicates sleepless nights, stress, anxiety, depression, nightmares. The Nine of Swords indicates some kind of pain that the Querent is going though. Often it speaks of worry, but that worry may be self-inflicted. The Querent is spending a lot of time and energy brooding about a problem, creating stress where perhaps there doesn't need to be any or as much. They may be blowing something out of proportion or they may legitimately have a difficult time on their hands. Either way, the need to relax and get a grip is inherent in this card. If the Querent is feeling guilty about something, they need to find a way to exorcise that guilt. Take responsibility, forgive yourself and move forward. Depression could also be indicated here.

If you see the Nine of Swords next to the Ten of Swords, Six of Swords, Three of Swords, problems are heavy indeed. If you see it next to the Star, things will get better or are getting better. Next to the Seven of Swords ID there's a sense of relief, something will be returned to the Querent such as their property, reputation or dignity, their peace of mind will be restored, a relationship will be back on track, wrongs will be righted.

III Dignified: the situation is getting out of hand, the depression is deepening, there could be thoughts of suicide or self harm. There is an inability to put things into perspective anymore and a sense of hopelessness. Contrarily, this card can also indicate that there is an end to their suffering; that bad times are nearly over. (Naturally the reader needs to assess not only the cards surrounding this one, but the state of the Querent as well.)

Next to the World, it can indicate that troubles are nearly over and that there's a light at the end of the tunnel. Next to the Two of Swords ID, a weighty decision has to be made and that decision is causing stress. The Querent may be reluctant to do the right thing as it is difficult or unpleasant in some way. Next to Justice, the anxious state the Querent finds herself in at this time could be the result of some behaviour she previously engaged in. She may need to accept responsibility for her actions.

The Nine of Wands
This card is about having the strength for the final push. It's important for the Querent to understand that the battle isn't over yet and that they will have to be prepared for more to come. These difficulties may be challenging but if the Querent is prepared, they will manage. Sometimes, the best way of fighting is not to fight at all, but to wait things out and see what will happen. This card indicates that it's important to have the wisdom to know exactly when to fight and when to be patient. If need be, defend yourself, and do it well. If you can get by

without it, then let things pass. The tides always turn.

If you see the Nine of Wands next to the Ten of Cups or the Nine of Cups, it's the achievement of the Querent's lifelong dream. Things are coming together. If you see the card near the Lovers, or the Two of Cups or the Four of Wands, it indicates that friends or lovers are somehow involved in this success. If you find the Nine of Wands next to the Six of Swords, remind the Querent that though times might be difficult now, they will get better and the rewards will be better than they imagined. They just have to hang in there.

III Dignified: this card can indicate a health problem. It can indicate a project which is failing because it's impractical or has been badly planned. It can indicate a wildly defensive attitude that turns people off. 'The best defence is a good offence', which has, in fact, become offensive. The Querent needs to hold their aggression in check, or if they are dealing with a person who is aggressive, they need to know the best way to deal with such an individual. This card can indicate that the Querent wants to give up, to walk away from their goals, but remind them that they are almost there.

If you see the Eight of Cups next to the Nine of Wands ID, it could indicate that the Querent may be fighting a losing battle. Ask them if they really think they can win, and if they do win, will it have been worth it. Next to the Two of Swords ID, it looks as though choices being made by the Querent have not helped the current situation and that in fact, they've only made things worse. Balance is needed.

If you see Strength next to the Nine of Wands ID, assure the Querent that they have the necessary energy to get through this, but that they will have to find that energy within themselves. Don't be afraid to ask for help.

The Nine of Coins

This card is about luxury, wealth, wisdom, all achieved through hard work and over time. The Querent may find they receive an unexpected sum of money, a settlement of some kind or a gift that gives them financial security. There is a sense of emotional balance here, one that has been achieved through trial and error. This card speaks of a person who has had many experiences and who has consciously learned from those experiences, applying the lessons learned in a careful and disciplined way in their daily lives. Their efforts have paid off. This is about gracious living, dignity, wealth and sensuality.

If you see the Nine of Coins next to the Three of Coins, hard work and diligence have resulted in a just reward. Next to the Ace of Wands or the Ace of Coins, a new project or opportunity could have excellent results. Next to the Eight of Coins or the Magician, there is the sense that hard work and an application of studies have resulted in some sort of fiscal or emotional reward.

Ill Dignified: it can indicate luxury that's gone overboard and is now decadence. It can mean someone is squandering their resources and throwing their money, their time and themselves away. Treating yourself cheaply or not respecting yourself can be indicated here. It can be about a person who performs (sexual or other) favours for people they do not care for in an attempt to fill an empty place inside. This card can indicate theft or a con game. It can talk about money earned not through hard work but as a result of swindling. It can also indicate that the time of luxury and high living is nearly at hand, having been delayed.

Next to the Three of Coins ID, the Knight of Swords or Wands ID, there is an indication of being deliberately misled about financial matters. Take heed. Next to the King of Coins ID, money matters have been allowed to get out of hand. The Querent needs to rein in their finances. Next to the Tower, financial challenges could get the better of the Querent if he's not able to get organised.

Tens

Overburdened

Discord

Illness

Martyr

Family

Tradition

Success

breaking point

The Ten of Cups

This card is indicative of good times, love, spending time with family, security and a lack of worries. There isn't much about the material world in this card. It's mostly about good feeling. It can be lasting happiness. It can indicate the good feeling that comes after forgiving someone or letting go of old traumas that held us back in our development. There's a sense here that this card calls us to embrace happiness, to unclench our fists and let ourselves enjoy what we have without looking for trouble and creating problems where there aren't any. This card can be about wish fulfilment or achieving a long sought after goal. It can indicate happiness within one's family or a loving and stable home.

Think of this card next to the Lovers; the Star; the Empress; the Two of Cups etc. and you get the idea of a true and lasting peace, or the start of a great relationship, bonding, spending quality time together and love between family, friends or lovers.

Ill Dignified: it can indicate discord, family problems, sudden, unexpected and negative reactions or actions from family members or someone close to the Querent. It can indicate a loss of friendship, a manipulation for personal gain, or the kind of happiness that comes at someone else's expense. It warns of something that looks good but is illusory and fleeting. Happiness doesn't come with a price tag and people who think that if they just have a bit more, or a bit better and it will bring them joy are in for a surprise when they find it doesn't.

Think of this card, ID next to the Empress, (ID) or the Queen of Swords, and you get the idea of a manipulating presence. Someone malevolent is pulling strings and watching people dance. Next to the Ace of Swords you might get an idea of the mental clarity that's needed to either understand or solve an emotional problem.

The Ten of Swords

This card can indicate some kind of exaggerated martyrdom, someone who makes noisy sacrifices so everyone will know how wonderful they are. It can also indicate sudden, negative events that take your breath away and leave you feeling destroyed. This can sometimes be the result of something the Querent brought on herself or the actions of another person. This card isn't about a careless action that hurt someone's feelings, this is deliberate and calculated to be as hurtful as possible. The good news is that this card is about hitting rock bottom and the only way to go from here is up. It might not seem like it but things are going to get better and life will restore itself, hopefully with new lessons having been learned and precautions taken in the future against this sort of thing.

The Ten of Swords next to the Seven of Swords gives one the idea that someone has said or done something very unpleasant and that they're going to be caught out or that the guilty party will be brought to light. If you see the Ten of Swords next to the Lovers ID or the Devil, there is the sense that a relationship is suffering and it's causing a lot of heartache. The Ten of Swords next to the Tower or Death means that the Querent is going to experience some serious changes in their life and that they should be prepare for things to get worse before they get better. The important thing to remember and to stress to the Querent is that they will get better.

III Dignified: the Ten of Swords can alternately be that problems aren't as bad as first imagined or they are way worse than originally thought. It can indicate serious illness, injury, accidents, attacks. It can indicate the problem has already happened and that now things are getting better slowly. It can indicate a violent change in one's life. It can indicate that that someone is carrying out their role of victim to an absurd and damaging extreme.

Next to the Queen of Coins ID, the Empress ID (or any of the court cards), there is the indication of an unstable and demanding person in the Querent's life (or possibly the Querent himself) who is the cause of discord. Next to the Four of Coins ID, a jealous and possessive relationship will reach a crisis point. Next to the High Priestess ID, someone is convinced people are out to get them, their paranoia is interfering in their lives.

The Ten of Wands

The Ten of Wands indicates a sense of being overburdened by responsibilities, having too much to do, being left to clean up someone else's mess. If the Querent is being put upon by others, it's time for them to delegate their responsibilities or to firmly say no. This card can indicate that carrying these burdens is, in fact, unnecessary, and that the Querent could (if they wanted) simply put down all that they're carrying around and walk away from it. We're not obligated to wear the problems other people give us or for that matter, those troubles we bring upon ourselves. It can indicate a situation where the Querent was left holding the bag or had to clear up debts accumulated by someone else.

If you see the Ten of Wands next to the Two of Coins ID you get the idea of a person who has lost all perspective and is no longer able to balance the demands of their work with other things in their life. The Ten of Wands next to the Magician could express a need to organise carefully and to apply diligence to all tasks, and that organisational problems and a lack of discipline are at the root of the Querent's issues.

III Dignified: this card can indicate an inability to delegate tasks which lead to a great deal of stress. It can indicate a situation that is entirely out of control now and that the Querent doesn't know if she's coming or going. Her time is not being used effectively and she's thinking "What do I do?" instead of doing something. This card can speak of a spoilsport who sets out to deliberately rain on your parade because of jealousy or envy. It can indicate lies being told to mislead the Querent.

Next to Temperance ID, it gives the idea that a person with some kind of addiction or destructive habit is wreaking havoc and causing problems for the Querent and is leaving her with a mess to deal with that she does not need or want. It could also indicate that the Querent is the person who's wreaking havoc in the lives of others. Next to the Two of Coins ID, someone living an unbalanced life is refusing to accept responsibility for their actions. Next to the Ace of Swords ID, confusion about what to do next has led to an apathetic, listless state.

The Ten of Coins

This card speaks about having reached financial success and security. It can be about inherited wealth or can indicate to the Querent that their financial problems are going to be solved. It can indicate the traditions of family, maintaining a status quo, the influence of parents and relatives on the Querent. It can be spiritual satisfaction, wisdom, the good advice and teachings of an older person, possibly a family member who passes on information that holds the Querent in good stead. There is a sense of stability here. This is a card that indicates a calm and stable domestic situation, good health, a free flow of energy.

If you see the Ten of Coins next to the Nine of Coins, there is a sense of something luxurious, probably money, or something of a sensual nature that leads to comfort. If you see it next to the Three of Wands, imagine that a new direction will yield a more than satisfactory result in the future. If you see the Ten of Coins next to the Six of Cups, it could indicate that someone from the past will arrive back into the Querent's life, bringing wealth, wisdom, happiness or love with them.

Ill Dignified: this card indicates a family tradition or influence that makes it difficult for the Querent to move forward or change. It can indicate a lack of financial stability or that this stability will be longer coming than anticipated. It can warn against the tendency to hang on to things too tightly as when we grasp it results in driving love/money/friends away.

Next to the Emperor ID, rigid thinking about how life should be lived no longer works and is causing difficulties. Next to the Chariot, something's got to give, and a break could be a relief. Next to the Magician ID, someone has long since held rigid beliefs or practiced doctrines which are not serving them or the others around them.

COURT CARDS

In the tarot deck, the cards called "court cards" are made up of the Pages, Knights, Queens and Kings. Some people, myself included, find court cards problematic to read because they are quite flexible in their interpretation. Court cards can indicate actual people in the Querent's life, the Querent themselves, qualities that people have (kind, autocratic, selfish, impulsive etc.) or they can indicate situations in the Querent's life or the lives of people close to them. It can often mean messages are coming in any form.

With this flexibility of meaning, it can be challenging to read the cards and find meaning without engaging in a dialogue with the Querent. If you find a court card in your spread that speaks about a person, it could be that this is the Querent him/herself, or that it is another person who has been on the Querent's mind or someone who will play a role in the Querent's life. It can be that the relationship between the Querent and the person indicated by the court card will change, shift or take on new meaning.

<u>Pages</u>

Intelligence

Childlike

Responsibility

Gossip

Childish

Rigidity

Creativity

deceit

The important thing to remember about Pages is that they are manageable. They can represent problems, but not necessarily of the life altering or tragic variety. If they are people, they are people who can impact your life, but not necessarily in a serious or permanent manner.

The Page of Cups (Person)

If we are speaking about a person in the Querent's life, the Page of Cups usually represents a child, or someone childlike. It can mean a child is going to be born. It can refer to a person who is dreamy, artistic, a bit unfocused, trusting, with a wild imagination and creative ability. This kind of person is hard to pin down; they always seem to be on the moon. They are generally quite gentle and harmless.

Ill Dignified: the kind of person being indicated here is someone childish as opposed to childlike. They can be selfish, impulsive, mean-spirited. They might have a tendency to lie and to deliberately create problems for others because of jealousy or envy, or simply a desire to cause troubles. They can be selfish, lack imagination and be moody and demanding.

(Situation) If the Page of Cups isn't about a person but a situation, it could refer to a need for more imagination and freedom in the life of the Querent. They have to loosen up and relax, use their imagination, get in touch with their spiritual side, practice more compassionate ways of thinking, be a little more loving. The Page is like the unconditional love of children and how we could all use more of that in our lives.

Ill Dignified: the Page of Cups can refer to a loss of joy in the Querent's life. It can be the lack of a sense of humour, compassion and fair-play. It can indicate that lies are being told, that someone is being deceived and that this deception is possibly going to be revealed. It can indicate there is some self indulgence taking place, that someone has a tendency towards being shallow and superficial. They may be indulging in lies and vicious gossip meant to hurt another person.

(Message) If the Page of Cups is about a message, it's often a message about love, relationships and joy. There could be a surprise meeting that leads to something wonderful.

Ill Dignified: the card indicates a message of trouble on the horizon. It can be that a lie is going to be revealed, gossip unveiled, the loss of love.

If you see the Page of Cups next to the Empress it can indicate a pregnancy. If the Eight of Wands appears next to the Page, you get the idea of a message, one of importance. The Page of Cups next to the Three of Coins ID indicates that there is a need to be more focussed on the task at hand.

If you see the Page of Cups ID, next to the Tower, it can mean that something is going to wreak havoc and cause some major tumult in the life of the Querent, if it hasn't already. The Page ID next to the Seven of Swords ID indicates that the Querent trusted someone who betrayed them.

The Page of Swords (Person)

If the Page of Swords represents a person, it's a person who possesses a great deal of mental and verbal dexterity. They are intelligent and watchful of the people around them. Their observations can be made from a detached place; they are students of human nature and enjoy watching the way people interact. They see the truth of a situation, no matter how much the truth has been diluted. Generally, the Page of Swords indicates an honest person, someone who is quite diplomatic and able to speak to people in a direct but careful way. It can indicate an emissary, an excellent negotiator, someone who's come to deliver some news, not necessarily of the good kind.

III Dignified: if the Page of Swords indicates a person, he or she may be an unpleasant person. He watches people but he watches them as a spy would. He indulges in gossip; can't keep secrets; has few personal boundaries. He's the person who comes to your house and then looks through all the cabinets in your bathroom and then tells people what he found there. He's a vicious gossip who may be twisting the facts to make them more interesting. He may be lying completely but often there's a kernel of truth to what he says. He's often two-faced and sneaky, sly and clever. He may like to stir things up just to watch and see what happens.

(Situation) If the Page of Swords indicates a situation or quality, it would be the need to see through the smoke-screen, to employ critical thinking, diplomacy, honesty and to be careful. It reminds us to observe people; we gain just as much from watching what people do as listening to what they say.

III Dignified: if the Page of Swords ID indicates a situation, it's to remind us of the damage of gossip. We must be careful what personal details we give out about ourselves. Information, once out in the ether, can't be concealed again. It can indicate there could be an unforeseen problem or event coming your way. It may indicate ill health or some kind of problem.

(Message) If the Page of Swords indicates a message (and this applies to both Dignified and III Dignified) it's not necessarily a message the Querent wants to get. It can be troubling or upsetting. That being said, it's important to remind the Querent that the Pages are manageable and that the problem will be an annoyance but not likely to be something devastating.

If you see the Page of Swords next the Seven of Swords, you get the idea that gossip has taken on a life of its own and that damage has been done (or is about to be done). Next to the Devil or the Lovers (III Dignified) there's a sense that gossip, rumour or interference from a third party is damaging a friendship or love relationship. Next to the Nine of Swords, you get the idea that there's some anxiety, depression and loss of peace of mind due to this problem.

The Page of Swords ID next to the Eight of Cups indicates an unwelcome piece of news. Next to the Eight of Cups ID, the Page of Swords ID can indicate that an individual has been harbouring a grudge and will take revenge if given the chance. Next to Justice ID, the Page of Swords ID can indicate that rumour has become fact in the minds of many and unfair judgements are being made.

The Page of Wands (Person)

If the Page of Wands indicates a person, it is a person of great energy, with plenty of creative ideas. He/she is verbal, witty and often funny. This person is very loyal, and though they may be hasty at times, they are unswerving in their loyalty and are faithful to their partners and friends. They are free-spirited, not concerned with money or material items. They move often and sometimes go where the wind blows them. They can lack focus and though they have the spark of idea, they sometimes lack the discipline to see a project through. This kind of person touches others with their enthusiasm and positive outlook.

Ill Dignified: if the Page of Wands indicates a person, it can be someone who everyone thought was loyal and faithful only to find out that they were in fact deceitful. It can indicate a person who behaves like a drama queen, someone who likes life to be theatrical and chaotic. This person can be superficial and selfish. It can be a person who has betrayed the trust of the Querent (or the Querent has betrayed someone else's trust), told a secret or lied.

(Situation) If the Page of Wands indicates a situation or quality, it could be the need to allow ideas to flow freely and not to be constantly thinking of reasons why something can't work, instead of finding solutions. It can indicate the need for more passion, creativity, embracing life and being open to trying new things and learning. It can indicate a move is about to be made, a new job, a new career.

III Dignified: and when speaking about a situation, the Page of Wands can indicate a move that is delayed. It is a lost opportunity, a loss of passion, a creative void, frustration, the feeling of being hemmed in by choices and trapped.

(Message) If the Page of Wands indicates a message, it's generally a good one. Even reversed, the message is rarely going to be a catastrophic event, but something delayed or somehow less than originally anticipated.

If you see the Page of Wands next to the Two of Cups, a loyal friend will help and inspire. Next to the Four of Cups, good times and celebration with friends are in store. Next to the Three of Coins, a spark of some kind will inspire an important project.

The Page of Wands ID next to the Six of Wands ID indicates delays and a possible loss of some kind. Next to The Chariot, a move or promotion may be delayed or blocked entirely. Next to the Moon ID, there is a sense that the Querent is being led up the garden path by someone who is not being honest with them.

The Page of Coins (Person)
If this indicates a person, it could be a young person who is very focused and responsible (especially if they seem too mature for their age). This person is

usually very goal oriented and may be very concerned with earning money or getting good grades. They may be overly rigid in their ideas. This person may forget to take time out and relax, and their focus and drive can be overwhelming for the people around them.

III Dignified: if the Page of Coins indicates a person, it is someone who is rigid, dogmatic and not a lot of fun at parties. It is someone who doesn't relate well to others and lacks a sense of humour and a sense of fun. It's a person who doesn't converse easily and can be hard to be around. They might be a generally good person but have few social skills. Then again, this person may have some rather ugly personal traits. They might be unfriendly and unkind. They might be superficial and think that the end justifies the means, even if it means stepping on others. In making money, they might bend the rules and forget ethics.

(Situation) The Page of Coins can remind the Querent that more focus is needed and that they should apply some more discipline in their finances, jobs, health regimes, diets etc. It could stand to remind the Querent to look after their health more rigorously.

III Dignified: when indicating personality traits or situations, it warns against greed and overspending. It speaks to the Querent of being overbearing, to relax a bit, to let up and enjoy life. Being too rigid is damaging. It can indicate a health problem. Remember, Pages are manageable, so if health issues are indicated, they're not necessarily serious.

(Message) If the Page of Coins speaks of a message it can be a welcome message about finances, health, or work. It can indicate a promotion or a raise in pay.

III Dignified: it can indicate negative news, a financial problem, job loss or problems in the workplace, a health problem of some kind.

If you see the Page of Coins next to the Nine of Coins, there may be an unexpected financial windfall. Next to the Magician, careful learning and discipline will have good results. Next to the Seven of Coins, more focus is needed; work harder if you want to achieve more.

If you see the Page of Coins ID next to the Ten of Cups ID or the Star ID, a desired outcome may not happen at this time. Next to the Ace of Coins ID, potential has not been reached. Start back at the beginning and try again, but more diligently this time.

<u>Knights</u>

Hurtful

Unstable

Passionate

frenetic

Old-fashioned

pedantic

Diplomatic

Selfish

Knights usually indicate young men but they can also represent women as well. Like other court cards, Knights can represent actual individuals in the Querent's life, the Querent themselves, situations, or personal qualities. They tend to be more dramatic in nature than Pages.

The Knight of Cups (Person)

If the Knight of Cups represents a person, he's likely to be young, most likely male with some dreamy qualities about him. He's passionate, romantic, not necessarily the most level headed individual. He can have a tendency towards blind loyalty even when that loyalty isn't warranted. He can be deeply hurt when and if he discovers the object of his love is a disappointment and can take things very personally.

Ill Dignified: he can be moody, with a tendency towards depression and he can be unstable, demanding and needy. This is a person who can almost literally suck the energy out of you. This is a high maintenance individual who will need a great deal of reassurance.

(Situation) If the Knight of Cups indicates a situation, it could indicate news is coming, usually of a romantic nature. It can indicate the start of a relationship or a marriage proposal.

Ill Dignified: it could indicate a relationship on the rocks, bad news coming, or someone using trickery and deceit. It could also indicate fraud.

(Quality) If the Knight of Cups indicates a quality in a person, it might be there to remind someone that they should surrender to their dreams now and again, that dreaming is a healthy and good thing to do and that it can help surmount the problems in life as well as solve problems creatively.

III Dignified: it could appear to remind someone that they are a little too dreamy, that they're not planting themselves firmly in reality and that they're in danger of getting carried away by pipe dreams. They need to get their feet back down to earth and then find a little balance between living in the real world and having their head in the clouds.

The Knight of Cups next to the Ace of Cups, the Two of Cups or the Lovers can indicate the start of a passionate romance. Next to the Star, the dream of a happy relationship is within reach. Next to the Two of Coins, kick back, relax and have some fun.

The Knight of Cups ID next to the Seven of Swords (Dignified or III Dignified) can indicate that someone is being dishonest. Next to Judgement, there is a sense that dishonesty and cheating will be found out. Next to the Three of Coins ID, a little less talking and more focus on work is needed.

The Knight of Swords (Person)

Where the Page of Swords deals with diplomacy, the Knight throws all that out the window. If he is a person, he is an individual who sees the world as very cut and dried. He considers everything in an unemotional way and can be hurtful to the people who love him not because he wants to be but because he doesn't see the value of speaking gently when the blunt truth will do. He is, however, an intelligent man (or woman) and capable of thinking with great clarity. He's not easily deceived and there is a kernel of compassion in him, buried deep. He may surprise you with an unexpected act of kindness.

III Dignified: he's an individual who uses his intellect to hurt others. He might start rumours and say ignorant things just for the joy of watching people get wound up. Careful of the things he says, he can be a very convincing liar, and he'll lie for no apparent reason other than his own amusement.

(Situation) If the Knight of Swords indicates a situation, it's often one that erupts quickly, a sudden event that shocks, something that happens quickly and unexpectedly. Usually, this event is not greatly welcome and can have an element of violence to it, physical or emotional.

III Dignified: the event is more serious, more harmful, more shocking. Steps can be taken to prevent this situation if the Querent is willing to work quickly. Honesty is key here, as the Knight of Swords (and Swords in general) promises swift retribution to those who lie.

(Quality) If the Knight of Swords indicates a quality in a person, it could be the need to think more critically, to act more decisively, to be less emotional and more practical. It reminds the Querent that you can't make an omelette without breaking a few eggs, so get on with it.

III Dignified: it says clearly that tact and kindness are in order, that just because you think something, doesn't mean you have to say it. It reminds the Querent to be on guard for arrogance and to watch the things they do and say because everything we do counts for something.

If you see the Knight of Swords next to the Six of Cups, the truth about something which happened in the past may be revealed. Next to the Hanged Man, if you distance yourself from a situation and simply reflect on it, the truth will be known to you. Next to the Emperor or Judgement, lies will not do. Tell the truth the first time and accept the consequences.

If you see the Knight of Swords ID next to Judgement ID, someone has been misinformed and is judging harshly based on that misinformation. Next to the Devil, a romantic relationship is being torn to shreds by unkind words or dishonesty. Next to the Moon ID, someone is being deliberately dishonest. They may be found out.

The Knight of Wands (Person)

If the Knight of Wands is a person, it's a young person who is the centre of attention, who loves to party, who has a gaggle of friends and who is always in the middle of frenetic action. This person has a lot of irons in the fire and despite a less than polished exterior he can be very warm and kind inside. This is a person who likes to rescue others and who feels the need to save people.

III Dignified: this person can be selfish, mean spirited, bossy or a bully. They take pleasure in having power over someone else and feeling as though they run the show. They like to feel powerful and can abuse that power. It can be difficult to have an individual like this in your life.

(**Situation**) If the Knight of Wands represents an event or situation, it's one of great importance, one that happens suddenly. This event will bring with it a good deal of change and though it might be sudden and a bit of a shock, it's often good news in the end.

Ill Dignified: that event can be quite negative in character. It is likely something brought on by neglect on the part of the Querent or a person close to them. A lack of care at work or at school will have consequences.

(**Quality**) If the Knight of Wands represents a personal characteristic, it could indicate the need to find more energy, to act more speedily, to be more spontaneous, to stand up for what is right and to put yourself on the line for things you believe and to systematically handle the challenges life gives you.

Ill Dignified: it can mean the need to back off a bit, that overwhelming energy can scare people, and that more planning might be necessary.

The Knight of Wands next to the Eight of Coins can indicate that a project will end in success if you work diligently. Next to the Four of Wands, a celebration will centre around a dynamic, young person. When you see the Knight of Wands next to the Hermit, it may be advisable to take a step back and consider carefully instead of plunging in without thinking.

The Knight of Wands ID next to the Fool indicates poor decisions taken quickly and without the appropriate information. Next to the Devil, it can indicate a person who is deliberately cruel to their friends or partner. Next to the Five of Coins ID, a rash decision will have serious consequences.

The Knight of Coins (Person)

If this is a person, it's a young person who can seem older than their years. This can be a person who has an old-fashioned outlook on life, who tends to hang on to older ideas. This person is incredibly reliable, decent and honest. If they say they will do something, you can absolutely count on them.

III Dignified: they can be pedantic, rigid and socially backward. They're so focused on the task at hand that they tend to forget about social grace. Though this person is not a harmful person per se, (that is, it is not their intention to harm others) they can be difficult and frustrating due to their rigid ideas and lack of diplomacy. They are likely the sort of person to "spill the beans" at an inopportune moment not out of a desire to be hurtful, but out of poor social aptitude.

(Situation) If this represents an event, it could be the need to take responsibility for something, perhaps an old mistake. It assures success if the Querent sticks with it and does the right thing. It could indicate a new job or more responsibility in their current job.

III Dignified: it means old mistakes could come back to haunt the Querent. If they shirked their

119

duties or sloughed their work off on someone else, the piper may come calling. If they made a mistake and then tried to cover it up, they could be found out.

(Quality) If this represents a quality, it's the need to organise thoughts, to plan carefully, and to go forward with good intentions. It reminds us that steady character is more important than flash and excitement and that an eye towards the future and on goals is always needed.

III Dignified: there's the danger of having become too rigid and a bore. The Querent (or someone close to them) needs to loosen up a little and enjoy themselves.

If you see the Knight of Coins next to the Nine or Ten of Cups, honest living and decency will have its rewards. Next to the World, past good deeds will be rewarded in unexpected ways. When the Knight of Coins appears next to the Six of Swords, a loyal friend will help you through a bad time.

The Knight of Coins ID next to the King, Queen or Knight of Swords can indicate that past dishonesty or bad behaviour will be exposed. Next to the Lovers ID or the Two of Cups ID, someone's harsh and unbending world view is taking the joy out of a relationship.

<u>Queens</u>

Intuitive

Strength

Generous

Unstable

Ambition

Suspicious

Maternal

Unethical

QUEENS

Like the other court cards, a Queen can be a quality reflected in the Querent (or someone close to them) or it can indicate a person. Generally, when referring to a person, Queens indicate women. It can also indicate a situation they find themselves in and possibly give some advice on how to deal with that situation.

The Queen of Cups (Person)

This can be a woman who is dreamy, not terribly sophisticated and a bit new-agey in some ways. She might be very maternal and caring and have or seem to have the ability to "see things". She might be described by people who know her as a bit odd in some way. She may say things that seem strange or out of place, she might make predictions that often seem to come true. She's good with children and people in general, a good listener. She's supportive and kind and often knows the right thing to say to make people feel better about themselves and the situations they find themselves in. She's intuitive and capable of compassion. She's a good friend.

Ill Dignified: the Queen of Cups is unstable. She may be convinced of her own psychic abilities which appear to be based on ego. She makes enemies and though you may not know what it is that you've done to upset her, be careful because she can be unpleasant in the extreme. She'll fight you at the back door, spreading rumours or influencing others but she won't come out into the open.

Situation / Quality If the Queen of Cups is a situation or a character trait, it's probably appearing to remind the Querent that they either need to be a bit more spiritual, compassionate, kind or possibly that they need to get their feet more firmly planted on the ground. It often serves to remind people that they know what the truth is already, and that they already know the right thing to do. In some decks, the cup the Queen is holding is closed with a lid. This could refer to secrets, to something hidden away but all you have to do is open up the cup and you'll see everything you need to.

This card can remind people about the need to listen to their instincts. Often listening to that little voice in your head tells you all you need to know about a situation, a person, a choice. The Queen of Cups is a road back into this instinct, but be aware that intuition is easily confused with ego. We often think we "know" something just because it serves our purpose and our egos or makes us feel better about something. It could refer to the birth of a child, a blossoming romance, the culmination of love of some kind.

If you see her next to the Empress, she can signify a feminine strength and wisdom. If you see her next to Justice, there's the sense that there's going to be some closure to a situation that will give all parties a sense of relief, that everyone will walk away feeling better than expected.

The Queen of Cups ID next to the Nine of Swords, the Three of Swords, the Tower indicates someone is meddling in the life of the Querent (or the Querent is the one doing the meddling) and it's going to explode. It's usually enough to gently remind these people that what you do comes back to you, and that plotting or rumour-mongering can create a monster that takes on a life of its own.

The Queen of Wands (Person)

The Queen of Wands can indicate a woman of strength. She lacks the dreamy qualities of the Queen of Cups, but what she lacks in ethereal charm, she makes up for in determination. She's direct, intelligent, often very educated and erudite. She has definite opinions and is more a leader than a follower. She is persuasive and convincing. She is often very scientific in her approach to things and this can lead people to think that she's unfeeling and without compassion, which may very well be the case. She may not be the most understanding person you will ever meet, but she gets things done and people listen to her. Often she has no children, or if she does, she's not very maternal. She can be very social and then suddenly retreat when she feels she needs some peace and quiet. She can be hard on her partners, alternately dominating them and treating them well. She can be unpredictable and at times difficult. Also unlike the Queen of Cups, she's very direct, and if she has a problem with you, you will know it. She can be very diplomatic, when she feels it's necessary. She can be very ambitious.

Ill Dignified: She can be very difficult and at times abusive. Her sense of humour can be sarcastic and cutting and she can say mean things under the guise of a joke. She can be overly sensitive, and see insult where none was meant. She rarely changes her mind and even more rarely forgives. She can be quite snobby and at times seems very judgemental, especially when she has the idea that someone isn't as intelligent as she is. People listen to her but probably not as much as she listens to herself. She may have had some past painful experiences, but she isn't likely to share them with you. If she is your Querent, she may not open up to you, making the reading that much more difficult.

Situation / Quality If this card represents a situation, The Queen of Wands can indicate a career being developed, a project being completed. This can often be something intellectual or public, such as politics, journalism, or acting. The Queen of Wands can speak of things that flow smoothly. A marriage or relationship that works nicely but contains no great passion.

Ill Dignified: it could be a blockage of some kind, some energy being wasted, spinning your wheels, a relationship or family situation that seems to revolve endlessly around the same issue, nothing changing, and probably never changing. This isn't to say it's a dramatic situation, it's probably not. Wands are not cards of great emotions. It's just a resignation that things are this way, and that's how they are.

If you see the Queen of Wands next to the Ace of Swords, for example, it can indicate a project which will have great intellect and power. Next to the Eight of Coins, you get the idea of a person who is methodical and careful, that they have a goal in mind and are working towards that goal, one hundred percent. Next to the Lovers, especially ID, you get the sense of a relationship dominated by the female partner.

If you see the Queen of Wands ID next to the Three of Wands ID, you get the idea that someone is being misled. Something is being deliberately misrepresented and with ill intent. The Queen of Wands ID next to the Six of Cups can speak of an intellectually powerful woman who seems trapped in the past somehow, and she's being diminished by her need to remember things gone by. Next to the Seven of Swords, it can indicate a woman who is able to use her intellect to mislead and hurt others. She's not above lying; she's making judgements and taking matters into her own hands.

The Queen of Coins (Person)

The Queen of Coins is a woman who is generous and practical. Though she may not have children of her own, she is nurturing. She is concerned with material matters and security, at times almost too much so. She is careful with money and may have a surprisingly large amount stashed away. She's good at investing and watches her resources with great care. She may seem like she doesn't have much, so don't be surprised if you discover that she's worth a lot more than you had originally thought.

Of all the Queens, the Queen of Coins is the most accessible. She is motherly, and if she does not have children, she looks after those around her. She is usually loving and warm, generous. If you step into her kitchen there will be a cup of tea waiting for you. She has kind words for everyone and is supportive. She can be creative, good at crafts, probably keeps a neat and tidy home. She looks after her health, and though she may not be flashy or beautiful in the plastic sense of the word, she does possess a certain quality of attractiveness, not necessarily sexy, but appealing. She is the consummate hostess and a welcoming person.

III **Dignified:** you will find the Queen of Coins to be suspicious. She's a person who is convinced that around every corner is someone waiting to con her, to take advantage of her, steal her money, trick her or make a fool of her. She's very worried about financial security, to the point where she seems obsessed by every penny. She oozes negativity and has a general disregard for humanity. She might have a great deal of money, and if she does, she'll make a point of telling people how much she has (or hinting at it) and then taunting her family members by holding it over their heads like a knife. (Be nice to me or you'll get nothing when I'm gone) A person like this will use their last will and testament as a slap from beyond the grave. They have fantasies of "getting even" with people who have wronged them, usually by watching that person suffer materially. Their houses may reflect their personality – crammed full of unused refuse they hang on to as though all this rubbish were the crown jewels (*it might come in handy one day, and besides, it's mine*). Their homes will show little warmth and love, mostly functional spaces which reflect this person's lack of creativity. Often they think that creativity and beauty are a waste of time. They can be envious of people who are creative and beautiful, and have little tolerance for other people's happiness. They like to tell you how much things cost and sometimes like to emphasise all the things they have and all the things other people don't.

Situation / Quality the Queen of Coins can indicate greater financial security. It can indicate that the Querent will receive an unexpected inheritance. There is a sense here of wise investments having been made. It can indicate a happy home or emotional satisfaction and good health.

III Dignified: the Queen of Coins indicates mistrust of the people around you: An imbalance of love/ money/ health. There is the sense here of a lack of generosity. It can indicate a home in chaos or health out of balance. There could be the indication of money problems. This can bring out negative emotions such as jealousy, possessiveness, avarice, greed etc.

Queen of Coins next to the Empress is an extra helping of creativity and material wealth. Next to the Ace of Wands, it indicates a project is going to yield good results. The Queen of Coins ID next to the Four of Coins or the Nine of Cups indicates greed, a possible loss due to holding on too tightly.

The Queen of Swords (Person)
She is the friend you want on your side and the enemy you hope you never have. The Queen of Swords is usually an accomplished woman, very sharp and very intelligent. She learns quickly from her mistakes and does not make the same error twice. She's got a high level of verbal acumen and great intuition. She has a nose for lies and distaste for liars in general. She delights in finding the truth and more in telling the truth, which she frequently does with little tact or regard as to how the truth might sound to people. She has a great memory for

facts and may seem to have a lot of knowledge about many obscure things. She reads a great deal and is a critical thinker. She tends to believe that her opinion is the correct one and may be arrogant about the beliefs of others. She probably has few friends who she holds up to impossibly high standards, but if she does like you, she will fight for you and be very loyal. If you make a mistake, she will tell you in no uncertain terms. She is often unable to separate what people do from what they are, and can judge someone based on one bad act or thoughtless comment. Forgiveness is not in her nature. She is not particularly warm or maternal. She is ethical, however and can be counted on to do the right thing.

III Dignified: she is another kettle of fish entirely. While still intelligent and sharp, the sorrows in her life become the excuses for her behaviour. She is not particularly ethical and likely to stab people in the back while smiling at them. She's a master of half truths and putting a seed in someone's ear without saying much at all. She indulges in vicious gossip, says mean and unkind things. She enjoys creating chaos for others, is vengeful and can be quite mean. If she thinks someone has wronged her or been disrespectful in some way, she will get even. She may bide her time, waiting for the perfect moment to strike, but she strike she will and it will take your breath away. She's not the enemy you want, she's formidable to say the least, and you'd do best to stay off her radar entirely.

Situation / Quality – The Querent must make a decision based on truth, not emotion. They need to focus with their minds, not their hearts. There is a

129

possibility they are being deceived and need to clear away debris unemotionally and without drama. Getting rid of dead wood.

III Dignified: she reminds the Querent to be wary, something unpleasant is coming, a setback, a lie, gossip or rumour that will wreak havoc. This is not an accident, whatever it is has been done deliberately and the Querent must work hard to correct the damage.

The Queen of Swords next to Justice can indicate a situation in which truth will prevail, this may or may not be a good thing for the Querent. If they've been messing about, they're about to get their just deserts. If the Queen of Swords is near the Tower or Death, some discovery of truth will shake the Querent's world and make rebuilding their lives necessary.

If you see the Queen of Swords ID next to the Five of Swords or the Empress ID, it can indicate that someone has turned against the Querent and is going to cause trouble.

<u>Kings</u>

Attractive

Compassionate

Predator

Tyrant

Secure

Honesty

Narrow-minded

Merciless

KINGS

As with Pages, Knights and Queens, Kings can indicate either a person in the Querent's life or a situation. The Kings tend to refer to older males or authority figures of some nature if they pertain to actual people. Kings embody the elements of rulers such as authority, experience, wisdom and control. Obviously, a King ID will portray the characteristics of a ruler who is not benign in nature.

The King of Cups (Person)

The King of Cups is an interesting figure. He's not as splashy as the Emperor or as dangerous as the King of Swords, but he's quite powerful in his own right. If he represents a person, he's an older male, usually someone attractive or sexy. This person may be married but that might not stop him from having love affairs. If he is single, he seems to gravitate towards married women. He can be romantic, worldly, intelligent, experienced. A relationship with the King of Cups can be a wonderful experience because he can make a person feel as though they are the centre of the universe. It can also be frustrating and sad because he holds back and can sometimes leave his partners wanting more love or commitment. He likes to hold the cards. He's often well travelled and has had many experiences. He's not an open person, and though he might seem warm and welcoming, kind and giving, if the Querent pays close attention, they will see that in fact the King of Cups manages to indulge very little information about his own feelings or motivations. He is a keeper of secrets and hard to pin down. People are often attracted to the King of Cups because he seems very calm and non-judgemental with a good sense of humour. He appears to be gentle and kind, and normally he is, but if he gets angry, it can be shocking.

III Dignified: this man is a whirlpool. He is the tortured artist, he believes himself to be misunderstood and treated badly by the world and that this gives him the license to maltreat others. He's thoughtless and doesn't care much about other people's feelings. He sees others as a means to an end. He can be a sexual predator, a dishonest business man, a cheating partner. If he is abusive in any way, it's usually through withholding of affection.

(Situation) If the King of Cups represents a situation, it's probably a harmonious relationship, a deepening desire to be a better father or husband, some kind of emotional satisfaction.

III Dignified: it could be that the Querent is being double-crossed by (or is double-crossing) someone or that someone in authority is against them in some way and wants to make their life difficult. Warn the Querent to be wary, this person is not someone easily dismissed or easily dealt with. They will need all their wits and diplomacy to avert disaster.

If you see the King of Cups next to the Ten of Coins or the Ten of Cups, there is a sense of a stable and happy family situation. Next to the Tower, should disaster strike, an older male figure will be central in helping the Querent.

If you see the King of Cups ID next to the Queen of Swords ID, there is the sense of a clash of the (overly) emotional and the (il) logical which will create an uncomfortable atmosphere. Next to the Star ID, the Querent has hoped for a deeper level of emotion or commitment in their relationship with an older male. It is not likely to happen.

The King of Wands (Person)

The King of Wands is the ideal ruler. A person with great compassion and respect for other, passion for his work, the strength of his convictions, the ability to see the difference between the easy thing and the right thing, a strong moral code. He can be impulsive and at times not particularly tactful, but he is usually right. This type of person can often be found in politics or law, a university professor or doctor. Usually he's an educated individual, accomplished and worldly. He's energetic and honest. The King of Wands is a great family man, he's loyal to his partner and involved in his children's upbringing. He's very concerned with disseminating the ideals of respect and discipline.

III Dignified: think of the King of Wands like a tyrant run amok. He's selfish, mean-spirited, interested in his own comfort and pleasure and not above watching people suffer while he sits comfortably. He can be ruthless in business, lying and being deceitful as he deems it necessary. He uses people. The Querent might be tempted to think that things will improve, and that given the right set of circumstances, this person will change and soften, become kinder and more generous. He won't. It's not in his nature. Some people are just born this way.

(Situation) If the King of Wands represents a situation, it's that it's time to take control of your life and move forward. Old ideas have held the Querent back, old prejudices and beliefs have become obsolete in light of new information. Once our eyes are opened up, we have no choice but to move forward. The King of Wands also indicates that the Querent should accept good advice.

III Dignified: it could be a level of dishonesty somewhere in the Querent's life that will come to a head. It could be that there is an abuse of power, that someone is being lied to or taken advantage of. If might indicate narrowness of mind and a bigoted and uncompassionate approach to life in general and people in particular. Depending on the cards surrounding it, the King of Wands reversed could indicate a misogynistic streak in a man, a hatred of women and a desire to be punishing.

If you see the King of Wands next to the Magician, discipline and careful application of work will result in recognition and reward. Next to the Two of Wands, having applied themselves, the Querent too will be able to reach a level of expertise and respect.

If you see the King of Wands ID next to the Tower, dishonesty and abuse of power will result in disaster. Next to Judgement or Justice, there could be an element of legal intervention if the law has been broken. Next to the Empress, a difficult marital relationship could be indicated.

135

The King of Coins (Person)

The King of Coins is an older man, almost always a person who is well off financially. He's not spectacularly smart or witty or bright, in fact you might think he's a little on the boring side, but he's materially successful. He is a clever investor and an intelligent business man. He knows that giving back is the door to receiving more. Although he's wealthy (or comfortable) he's not given to bragging about his wealth or being obvious with it. He's just as likely to live simply but with excellent quality. He doesn't have a big temper and isn't a vengeful sort of person, but if pushed a long way, he will cut people out of his life and never have anything to do with them again. He's not forgiving, especially if he thinks people have been disloyal.

Ill Dignified: the King of Coins can represent a person who cares more about money and the acquisition of money than anything else. He can be unscrupulous in his dealings, almost dangerous. Often he can be involved in unethical, even illegal ways of earning money. He might be a con artist and be adept at tricking vulnerable people out of their fortunes. Mainly he is greedy, selfish and narrow-minded.

(Situation) If the King of Coins represents a situation, it's that it's time for the Querent to get their material affairs in order. They don't need to take great risks, but they do need to carefully examine the way they want to live versus the way they currently live and map out a plan on how to reach their goals. It can also be a reminder for the Querent that there is a time to give back to the community, that success comes with responsibilities and that giving and receiving are two sides of the same coin.

III Dignified: the Querent is reminded that the pursuit of material wealth is fine, but that they also need some balance in their lives. Loss of perspective about the importance of money will bring only sorrow and isolation. It could also be that the Querent or someone close to them has been spending recklessly without regard for reality, and that it's time to get themselves sorted out.

If you see the King of Coins next to the Nine of Coins, hard work will pay off financially. Next to the Four of Wands or the Two of Cups, financial stability will lend itself to celebration and a better emotional state. Next to the Seven of Coins ID, past lessons about waste and failure to apply ones self have been learned.

If you see the King of Coins ID next to the Two of Swords, a difficult decision will have to be made regarding a relationship with an older (unstable) male or a negative financial picture. Next to the Star ID, hoping that someone will change their ways is futile. You must learn to deal with the situation or person as they are.

The King of Swords (Person)
The King of Swords is an older male, he's best suited for a career as a judge or law maker. He's able to make decisions based on fact rather than on emotion and isn't an empathetic character at all. His decisions are usually correct. He can't stand corruption; he is a natural leader but not a great lover of humanity. He can not be bribed and shows

no mercy to people who he feels are corrupt or who have been dishonest. He commands respect but not love. His lack of compassion for others can be misleading, he may not be the cold person everyone thinks he is (or perhaps he is) but he has some other qualities that make up for it. If he believes in something, he will put himself on the line trying to put it into action. He is not a forgiving person, he's severe at times.

Ill Dignified: he can be a person without mercy. He appears to be utterly unkind and without compassion. He may demonstrate an utter disgust for people who he considers to be weak or beneath him. He can be a tyrant, his judgement can be wildly unfair. He'll lie, steal, hurt people and not seem to be at all affected by what he does.

(Situation) If the King of Swords represents a situation, it could be that the Querent needs to find some backbone and be courageous. It might be time to stand up for what they believe in and do the right thing. It could be that a decision must be made and the King of Swords reminds the Querent to think with their head and not to be swayed by emotional arguments. It reminds us that we need to stand up for what we believe in rather than slink away from a challenge. New ideas need to be looked at more carefully.

Ill Dignified: it can be the warning of an unfair judgement directed towards (or made by) the Querent. It can be a reminder of harsh prejudices that serve no one and hurt others. It can warn of trouble coming down the pipes, the Querent needs to prepare themselves for some ugly possibilities.

If you see the King of Swords next to the Nine of Swords, it is only the Querent who holds herself back. She has the courage to do what needs to be done, even if she thinks she doesn't. Next to the Five of Swords ID, the Querent knows that lies are being told and in her heart, she knows what to do about it.

If you see the King of Swords ID next to Justice or Judgement, decisions are being made that are not necessarily just nor are they in the Querent's favour. Next to the Five of Wands, it may be necessary to fight for what is right. Next to the Magician ID, there is an element of trickery here. Someone is not being honest.

MAJOR ARCANA

The Major Arcana are the twenty-two cards which go from the Fool to the World. They symbolise important journeys, significant changes and lessons in the life of the Querent. The Fool is the first card in the Major Arcana and he represents innocence and a lack of knowledge. He is a fool not in the sense of stupidity but in the sense of being a complete beginner. He begins his journey naive and trusting and learns lessons along the way, gradually maturing until he reaches the World, the last card of the Major Arcana where he finds his goals reached and his dreams fulfilled. Along the way he learns important lessons. The Major Arcana represents the lessons we all need to learn if we are to mature and become well-rounded and balanced adults.

THE FOOL

Innocent   naïve
Folly

The Fool is the first card of the Major Arcana. His number is zero. He literally represents starting from scratch, being new at anything, being untried, untested and inexperienced. He contains a sense of optimism and excitement, an attitude of hopefulness and sincerity that can carry him through. It can also get him into trouble if he doesn't pay attention to his surroundings or read between the lines more closely. The Fool often indicates the Querent herself, and can appear at a time when she finds herself starting something new, a new relationship, a new job, a new way of thinking. It embodies the ideas of being spontaneous and adventurous, of making big decisions, of allowing yourself to look foolish if that's what's necessary. The cards next to the Fool will give you a clue in what area the Querent finds themselves in new waters.

Next to the Lovers, the Fool indicates relationships, the Ace of Swords or Wands could indicate business projects; any number of Coins could indicate a new home or increased wealth.

III Dignified: the Fool indicates folly, decisions being made without thought or planning; a lack of experience leading to problems. People who don't know what they're doing suddenly find themselves with the keys to the kingdom are likely to wreak havoc and create problems. It could indicate bad decisions and a series of thoughtless acts leading to a difficult time. Sometimes it indicates no decision being made at all. A person who starts but does not finish projects, promises broken, compulsive behaviour such as gambling or drinking.

If you see this card next to Temperance, it could give an indication of an addiction or some kind of extreme behaviour. Next to the Nine of Wands it gives the idea of a Querent who finds themselves immobile, apathetic and unable to make a move. No move is, in fact, a decision in and of itself, and that to abdicate responsibility is to let someone else make a decision for you, and not necessarily one that you might like.

Slippery Dedicated

If this card indicates a person, it is a person of great skill. They are clever speakers and are convincing. They might be doctors or salesmen, scientists or politicians. They are active, energetic, believable and powerful. If the card indicates a situation, it usually indicates a high level of skill. It speaks of having done all the work necessary to achieve goals and in the process having educated and armed oneself with the information and skills necessary. It can indicate learning and especially discipline. This card can come up to remind the Querent of the things they need to do in order to get where they want to go. It can remind them not to lose sight of their goals and most importantly, that sacrifices must be made in order to get what they want.

If you see the Magician next to the Three of Coins, you see the idea of hard work and careful preparation coupled with discipline and learning to complete a project. Next to the Nine of Coins, for example, it speaks of the rewards of all this hard work, namely a good income.

III Dignified: the card can indicate a level of apathy, a lack of discipline, laziness, a person whose verbal skills are being used to manipulate people. Being stolen from, being conned. It can indicate someone who started out on a path to learning or achievement, but who has simply stopped and is doing nothing. It can speak of losing your way. It can sometimes indicate problems studying or learning.

Next to the Ten of Wands, you have the idea of being overburdened, which can lead to inertia and delays. Next to the Nine of Swords, there is the idea of apathy leading to the feeling of being trapped. If you see the Magician ID next to the Seven of Swords, there is the idea that someone is being conned, that a person with power and skill is using that power to manipulate others for their own means.

THE HIGH PRIESTESS

Intuitive Manipulator

The High Priestess can indicate a woman (usually older) who seems to have "psychic abilities" and who keeps many secrets. She relies heavily on intuition. Where the Magician tends to be open and teaching others, the High Priestess tends to be closed. In fact, she can be a keeper of secrets, revealing them one at a time, if at all. She may seem weird or flaky. If she indicates a situation, the High Priestess invites the Querent to open their mind to experiences that may seem strange to them. They may find themselves having dreams or receiving visions or signs, tell them that they should listen to these instincts and not to block these ideas when they come up. The Qualities represented by the High Priestess are wisdom, intuition, purity, duality of the feminine and masculine, ancient learning, spiritual and religious learning, secrets of all kinds.

Next to the Six of Cups, it could indicate a secret about the Querent's past that will come up, an old friend or acquaintance will arrive suddenly with a message. If you see the High Priestess near the Nine of Swords,

143

the answer to a mystery could give the Querent a sense of peace, setting them free from the bonds that have held them.

III Dignified: the High Priestess can be a person who acts as though she has secrets, who manipulates people by false claims. She may be posing as a psychic or a spiritual leader; she may be taking advantage of those who are more vulnerable because of their need to believe and to be led. It can indicate that things are not always what they seem, and that the Querent must pay close attention to the things going on around them to who they surround themselves with. There is the possibility they are being conned. The High Priestess ID can also indicate ignorance, a lack of learning, a narrow viewpoint. It may predict the exposure of a secret long thought buried, one that could cause potential problems.

If you see the High Priestess ID next to the Six of Swords, it could indicate that such a secret or such a person can cause the Querent to have some difficulties. Next to the Tower, the High Priestess has knowledge that when revealed will upset the Querent's world.

THE EMPRESS

Love   Instability

Is the embodiment of the feminine ideal. By this I mean not just traditional idea of the role of wife and mother, but the idea of abundance, creativity and love. She can indicate a marriage, or an engagement is forthcoming

144

or a relationship is about to blossom. There is the indication here of a happy, secure home life. It could indicate pregnancy or the birth of a child. It could also be a creative and artistic projection coming to fruition. She can indicate anything having to do with creation or creativity. There is also a sense of richness, not of the financial variety, but of the emotional variety. If the Empress is a person in the life of the Querent, she is a very good person to know. She's an excellent and loyal friend and a great listener. She is nurturing and kind. Though this card is usually read as representing a woman (if it refers to a person and not a situation) that is not necessarily the case all the time.

If you see the Empress next to the Page of Cups, it can indicate a pregnancy. Next to the Lovers: a relationship which is growing. Next to the Three of Coins, a work-related project which blossoms.

III Dignified: the Empress is the feminine ideal gone wrong. It can indicate an unstable person or family life. It can talk about an egotistical individual who strangles the others around her (or him) with neediness and demanding behaviour. It can speak of difficult or negative emotions, insecurity and difficulty. It can indicate financial issues or problems at home. There could be fertility issues such as an inability to conceive, miscarriage or a pregnancy at a bad time. It could be representative of a relationship falling apart. There could be a lack of creative energy or a project falling through, especially one that had shown promise at the outset. There are indications in this card of jealousy, envy, possessiveness, smothering or bad parenting. If this is a person, it is an obnoxious person who is not well liked.

Next to the Devil, a relationship falling apart amidst a great deal of fighting and arguing. Next to the Ten of Cups, it could indicate problems at home, or a delay in reaching desired goals. Next to the Two of Swords, decisions are being clouded by ego or bad feelings. Emotions are running high and more logic needs to be applied.

THE EMPEROR

Authoritarian Volatile

He is an authoritarian figure, lacking an excess of emotion. He rules largely from the head and demands loyalty. He likes to be obeyed without question and wants discipline. Though he prefers old fashioned values, he can also be flexible enough to see the world is changing. He's an excellent leader and an able judge of character. He is a good teacher. He can be unemotional almost to the point of seeming cold, but he is fair. He is responsible and capable. As a situation, he reminds the Querent to shoulder their responsibilities, to keep their word and to be fair in their dealings. It reminds them to judge situations more carefully, to be honest and decent. It can indicate the responsibilities of fatherhood. It can also indicate some kind of encounter with an authority figure or a government agency. Depending on the cards around it, this encounter may or may not be successful.

If you see the Emperor next to the Eight of Coins, it gives the idea that self-discipline and action will lead to satisfaction. Next to the Nine of Cups, it tells the

Querent that current activities, when managed carefully and honourably, will yield great rewards. Next to the Knight of Swords, it can indicate the need to be verbally dexterous, to convince people in order to lead them.

III Dignified: the Emperor is like Henry the Eighth at his worst. He's volatile, pleasure-seeking, vengeful and petty. He can be selfish and untrue. He's not beyond lying to get what he wants. I le may choose favourites and be very obvious about them to the detriment of others. He spends too much money and expects others to provide for him. He's a difficult man, a potentially violent or abusive father; he's a disciplinarian without love or affection. As a parent or family member, the Emperor ID is particularly frustrating – you can work very hard to win his love or approval but to no avail. It's important for the Querent to understand that what you see is what you get with the Emperor. There are not likely to be any hidden depths of emotion, no enlightened moments to be had where hands are held and love is expressed. As a situation, it could remind the Querent that they haven't been responsible, that they need to step up and take better care of themselves or their loved ones. It could indicate an unfavourable encounter with authority such as the government or the law.

Next to Justice, you can see that the Querent may not come out of this encounter the winner. Next to the King of Wands ID, you get the idea of abuse of authority without reason. The Querent will have to step lightly and try to extricate themselves from entanglements with this person.

Traditional
Judgemental

The Hierophant can indicate tradition, someone seeking knowledge and spiritual guidance. The Hierophant often appears when the Querent knows the right thing to do but is too reluctant (or lazy) to do it. He also seems to appear when the Querent is ready to learn something new or to embark on a new way of thinking. The Hierophant is not only the voice of your conscience, but the voice of spiritual reason. He can indicate a willingness to learn, to make good decisions, to give or receive sound advice or to engage in moral behaviour. The Hierophant can literally be interpreted as a teacher, as a person, usually an older male who may in fact be a teacher or priest, or a person who has given advice or direction to the Querent. He may be wise and supportive having had many experiences in life, but also having chosen a path that stresses goodness, and some form of values.

If you see the Hierophant next to the Three of Coins, a disciplined approach to work can bring recognition and the possibility of reward from a superior. Next to the Seven of Coins (especially ID) it indicates that the Querent has been shirking responsibilities and they must take more care. Next to the Nine of Swords, the advice or counsel of another person should be taken in order to ease the Querent's stress.

III Dignified: the Hierophant can be narrow-minded, judgemental, harsh in his opinions, unforgiving. He can represent bad advice or bad decisions that may come to haunt the Querent later on. Often, the Hierophant appears ID when the tune has been played and now it's time to pay the piper. In other words, the Querent may have engaged in some activity and now finds that there are consequences which need to be dealt with.

If you see this card III Dignified next to Judgement (especially if that is also reversed) the Querent could be facing some serious repercussions for past wrongs. Next to the King of Wands ID, it gives the idea of a tyrannical personality who wants everyone to step into line, someone punishing. Next to the Two of Coins ID, a lack of balance in the past will result in current problems. Seek counsel.

THE LOVERS

Attractive Jealousy

This is a card most often associated with sexual relationships and that's most often the case but not always. The Lovers appears when the Querent has embarked (or is about to embark) upon a relationship. It usually suggests harmony and great emotion but there can also be an element of difficulty in this card in the form of a difficult decision needing to be made. If the Querent has recently started a relationship, it could indicate that this will be a loving and rewarding union, harmonious and peaceful but not effortless. It's essential that the Querent and his or her partner both be facing in the same direction, that they want the same things from life and from each other in order to make their relationship a good and lasting one.

If you see the Lovers next to the Two, Four, Ace, Ten or Nine of Cups, it gives the idea of a joyful union built on a solid foundation. Next to the Three of Wands ID or the Three of Coins ID, the relationship can be rewarding but will require work on the part of the Querent and their partner. Next to the Six of Cups ID, a past love could be in contact, or the Querent still has feelings for a relationship which is now finished.

III Dignified: the Lovers can indicate the end of the party, a relationship beset by jealousy, anger and negative emotions. Things are winding down and perhaps the Querent doesn't want to admit it. There are problems in the relationship. Perhaps it can be salvaged but that depends on two people wanting to do the work necessary to make things better. It's hard to admit that things aren't so rosy and that the boat is leaving without you. Most of us make the mistake of associating our participation in a relationship with our self-worth. If we're alone we feel as though we are less and so we do what we can to hang on to something that should be let go of.

If you see the Lovers ID next to the Nine of Swords, a relationship has hit a bad patch and it's causing anxiety for the Querent. Next to the Three of Swords, it could indicate that the relationship is on its last legs. Next to the Five of Swords, there is the idea that the Querent or his partner is given to deliberately cruel behaviour. Next to the Devil, this relationship is now more one of mutual dependency and the joy has long since been wrung out of it.

THE CHARIOT

Movement Stagnation

The Chariot is usually used only to describe a situation. It can indicate movement, decisions that need to be made. It can literally be a move to a new home or a new job. It can indicate that the Querent must get her life under control, mastering her problems and emotions. It can indicate a hard-won victory, vindication, and vengeance upon one's enemies. It's a card of substance over emotion. It's more about planning and control than about joy or excitement. This card sometimes appears to remind the Querent that they must be more proactive in their lives and that they need to start planning carefully, stop leaving things to chance and to get their lives together.

If you see the Chariot next to the Three of Wands, a move to a new location could be work related or there could be a promotion in the works. Next to the Magician, hard work has paid off and will result in some kind of reward. Next to the Eight of Cups, a decision to leave behind things which no longer serve the Querent will ultimately result in a move forward.

III Dignified: it can indicate a delay in decisions, that a journey will be beset with problems, that a move will be problematic, delayed or cancelled altogether. It can indicate selfish behaviour and a disregard for other people. There's the general idea of delay or problems, but these can be serious. It can indicate unbalanced

151

behaviour on the part of the Querent (or someone near her) which is going to have a very negative effect. It can indicate that a loss of control is going to cause serious issues.

Next to the Five of Wands, the hoped for promotion or recognition in the workplace is farther off than originally thought. Take care that no one is sabotaging your efforts. Next to Temperance, extreme behaviours or laziness is getting in the way of the Querent's ability to move forward. Next to the Ace of Cups ID / the Lovers ID, the Two of Cups ID, a soured relationship is affecting the Querent's ability to progress.

STRENGTH

Control weakness

Strength is a card which refers to inner strength and less about physicality. It's also important to distinguish between strength and control. Strength is about self control, patience and calm, believing in yourself and going about your business with little flourish. Control is about getting people around you to fall in line because you want them to. Ego does not equal strength, and that sometimes the hardest thing to do is just to let people be what they need to be instead of imposing your will on them. It can indicate a future test of will, some kind of crisis or problem that will draw on all the Querent's resources.

Strength next to the Lovers ID indicates that a relationship will / has arrived at a point where extra patience and work are needed. Next to the Moon, depression, sadness or confusion has set in; remain as strong as possible to see your way through this time. Next to the Nine of Swords, the Querent's resources are being attacked by anxiety and worry. Hang in there.

III Dignified: the Querent is feeling weak and depleted, possibly after dealing with a great deal of problems. There's a lack of balance and they are suffering. They need to be reminded that it's ok to take some time out to sort themselves out, but after that they are probably going to have to get back into the battle. It can also indicate that the Querent or someone near them is behaving either like a bully or a weakling and draining the energy of those around them.

Next to the Ten of Coins, Strength ID could indicate family problems. Next to the Page of Swords, an individual who spreads rumour and gossip is chipping away at the Querent's resolve. Next to the Six of Coins ID, nostalgia for the past has turned into something more than fleeting thoughts. Obsession with things gone by will not help the Querent in the here and now.

THE HERMIT

Withdrawal   Isolation

This card usually indicates a need on the part of the Querent to look within themselves. There is a time we all reach when we simply need to withdraw in order to find what we seek. It could be that the Querent's social life or work environment is becoming toxic and it would be well-advised to stay as far as possible from the eye of the storm. Often this card comes up when the

Querent has been living their life at a hectic pace, never pausing to reflect on anything in their lives. The Hermit can also serve as a reminder that it is better to distance yourself from people who do not make you want to be a better person. Honest self-examination is vital.

Next to Temperance, the Querent or someone near them has engaged in some risky behaviour. Distance yourself now in order to avoid permanent damage. Next to the Three of Coins ID, someone in a work/school setting has been exaggerating their importance and is about to cause trouble. It could be necessary to distance yourself from them. Next to the Five of Coins (especially ID) the Querent should take some time to realise how they got into the predicament they find themselves in and realise the need to keep away from chaos, and to reach out and ask for help.

III Dignified: it can indicate a prolonged period of isolation that is leaving the Querent (or someone close to them) feeling unbalanced and sad. It can indicate some kind of deep depression or exaggerated isolation. It can remind the Querent of the need to get back into an active life. In extreme cases, the Hermit ID can indicate loneliness or thoughts of suicide. It could be that this isolation is, in fact, not the Querent's choice but is being imposed upon them by a domineering individual in their lives.

Next to the King or Queen of Cups, the Lovers, the Six, Four, Two or Ace of Cups, this isolation could be due to some romantic relationship having gone bad. Next to the Nine of Coins ID, there is a financial element to the isolation. Perhaps a recent job loss has resulted in shame, separating the Querent from their old social group. Next to the Queen of Swords ID, the Emperor

ID, the King of Wands ID, the Querent is being bullied by someone more powerful than they are.

THE WHEEL OF FORTUNE

Change Problems

The Wheel of Fortune was a popular medieval concept. It embodied the idea that each of us is on a big wheel going up like a Ferris wheel at the fair. We reach the top (where we experience success, wealth, love, happiness) and inevitably we come down again, crashing down, in some cases. This card often comes up as a hint that there are some big and not necessarily pleasant changes ahead. It serves to remind us that life runs in cycles and that we must always strive to be of good character. If, when we reach the top of the cycle we behave arrogantly and imperiously, we will not be offered any assistance by people we have snubbed or been unkind to when our lives were easier. As much as we'd like to think it's not possible, it can happen to us. If the Querent has been enjoying a period of prosperity and happiness, they may experience some obstacles. If they've been depressed or unhappy and having a run of bad luck it can indicate that things are going to get better. How extreme the cycles are depends almost entirely on how the Querent lives their life.

Next to the Seven of Coins ID, there could be some financial issues ahead. Caution is needed. Next to the Eight of Coins, the Magician, the Three of Coins, hard work will pay off. Next to the Lovers, the Devil, the Ace, Two, or Four of Cups, a relationship will experience a change, either for good or for ill.

155

III Dignified: this card can either be an intensification or a delay of this impending change. If the Querent has been behaving badly, they'd best be prepared for the consequences. Again, they are reminded that for every person they were unkind to on their way up, they could experience equal treatment on their way back down. The less extremely you live your life, the less these cycles will shock and demean you.

Next to the Seven or Five of Swords, or the Five of Wands, arrogant or cruel behaviour has some unexpected and unpleasant consequences. Next to the Three of Wands ID, plans are going to be changed or fail to come through. Take care in business dealings that all parties involved are knowledgeable and honest. Next to the Four of Coins ID or the Nine of Cups ID, jealousy or possessiveness has provoked a loss of some kind.

JUSTICE

Retribution reward

Everything you do or don't do comes back to you at some point. The words we say, the actions we take, the things we do when we think no one is looking. If the Querent has been wronged by someone, there will be some kind of justice, retribution, vengeance, vindication, etc coming their way. It serves to remind us that we need to be careful with our actions as what goes around, comes around. This card can also literally deal with justice, encounters with the law, with police, judges, etc. If the Querent has been deceitful and fears being exposed, this card may indicate that exposure is at hand, or has already happened. In this case, the Querent may do well to confess ahead of being caught out. Whatever the case, they must be prepared to accept the consequences.

Next to the King of Wands ID or the Emperor ID, this will be a punishment far worse than the crime. Next to the Ten of Cups/ the Magician, the Eight of Coins, the dreams of the Querent are at hand. Hard work has paid off and they will get what they deserve. Next to the Seven of Swords, something taken from the Querent (or taken by the Querent) will be returned to its rightful place.

III Dignified: it can be justice perverted or corrupted. It can indicate bad people getting away with their actions while good people pay. It can indicate a punishment much harsher than the crime. It can also mean justice will be delayed, perverted or blocked entirely.

Next to the Empress ID, the matter could be of an emotional nature and may not end well. Next to the Seven of Swords (Dignified or III Dignified) lost property may not be returned and the perpetrators may get away with what they have done. Next to the Nine of Swords (Dignified or III Dignified), there can be the indication that a delay in justice or justice abused is causing stress for the Querent. Next to the Four of Swords, non-action on the part of the Querent will have an unpleasant result.

THE HANGED MAN

Wisdom   frenzy

157

This card reminds us of the need for stillness and calm. It reminds us about the need for solitude, searching for answers and taking time out to nurture the spiritual side of our natures. This card sometimes comes up when the Querent is living a life that involves as little thinking as possible. It can remind us of the need to take ourselves out of the race once in a while. Wisdom cannot be achieved at a thousand miles per hour nor can it be achieved by blindly following the words of others. It can indicate that if the Querent only stops, listens and observes, they will have all the answers they seek.

Next to the Seven of Swords, the Three of Wands ID, the Five of Wands ID, the Querent has some tiny suspicion about the intentions or truthfulness of someone in their life. If they only agree to sit back and observe, they will know everything they need to know. If the Hanged Man appears next to the Six of Cups, reflection on the past may reveal previously unknown answers. Next to the Two of Swords, a difficult choice requires the Querent to withdraw and seriously consider their options. If they let themselves be still and observe, the right answer will come to them.

III Dignified: the Querent is not in the habit of keeping still long enough to contemplate or relax. Their frantic or busy lifestyle leaves little room for calm and this could have some repercussions down the road. In order to clearly see what is going on in our lives, we need to be able to stop, take a breath and observe without comment. It could also indicate that the Querent has taken stillness and solitude to an extreme which is now harmful to them.

Next to the Fool ID, the Querent has made a series of unwise choices that have led to chaos. Inability and inexperience have led to problems. Next to the Lovers ID, a lack of discrimination when choosing a partner has led to a relationship that is not working on many levels. The Querent needs to observe their partner more closely in a realistic, dispassionate way. Next to the Page of Swords ID, there is an element of vicious gossip or rumour being spread or a person in the Querent's life who is deliberately making mischief. The Querent has not been paying attention previously and needs to stop and take a look at what is going on around them.

DEATH

 Change

The appearance of this card has an immediate gut reaction in a Querent, usually one of fear. Although this card can literally indicate a physical death, it is important to remind the Querent that it is also about change, transition, old things going away to make way for the new. Relationships, friendships, jobs, projects, each of these can shift, change or simply cease to be. The Death card can indicate any of this. It can also indicate the death of an old way of living or thinking in order to make room for a new philosophy. Death is just another transition but it's the one we instinctively fear most.

Next to the Ace of Coins ID, remind the Querent of the need to take care of themselves. Regular medical check-ups are advisable. Next to the Ace of Cups ID, the Lovers ID, the hoped for love relationship may not turn out to be everything that had been hoped for. Next to the Five of Coins ID, stubbornness and a refusal to seek help on the part of the Querent will result in doors being permanently shut to him. Next to the Six of Cups ID, longing for a relationship long since passed is nothing but detrimental to the present.

III Dignified: it can mean that a change in the Querent's life has been delayed or intensified. It could be sudden and rapid change. It could indicate that health issues are going to come to a head. A problem (medical, personal, financial etc.) previously ignored is now going to resurface and be harder to deal with than if the Querent had dealt with it when it first arose.

Next to the Three of Coins ID or the Three of Wands ID, there could be trouble in the workplace. Next to Justice, a decision hoped for will either be delayed or will not go in the Querent's favour, or if it does, it will not bring the satisfaction she had hoped to have. Next to Temperance ID, there is the sense that someone's extreme or addictive behaviour is going to catch up with them. Next to the Ten of Coins ID, there is the possibility of illness; the Querent should take care to have regular medical check-ups.

Balance addiction

Again, the need for balance appears. Temperance is a card that often appears when the Querent or someone in their life has been behaving in an extreme fashion. It can often indicate some kind of addiction, drugs, alcohol, food, sex, gambling, etc. There's a lack of balance and it's about to create some serious problems unless it's addressed as soon as possible. The Temperance card serves to remind us that moderation in all things is key.

Next to the Four of Wands ID, the Querent has been enjoying himself a little too much lately. It's time to rein this impulse in and plant his feet firmly on the ground. Next to the Devil (especially ID) there could be some drug or alcohol abuse in the background. Next to the Moon, depression or extreme emotional upset is fueling unhealthy behaviours. Next to the Tower, a lack of balance and moderation is the cause of calamity in the Querent's life.

Ill Dignified: the behaviour is getting out of control and is causing serious issues. It could be that someone is lying in order to cover up the extent of their extreme behaviour. A lack of balance is causing waves in the Querent's life. Steps need to be taken to get things back into alignment or the consequences could be dire. Hidden addictions could be indicated here.

Next to the Seven of Swords ID, it could be that someone is stealing from the Querent in order to fund their extreme behaviour. Next to the Star ID, someone is longing for something completely out of reach and is willing to do anything to reach their goal, no matter how unrealistic. Next to the Eight of Cups ID, the Querent knows very well the need to walk away from the situation but is finding it nearly impossible to do so.

THE DEVIL

Jealousy Abuse

The Devil is another card that invokes an emotional reaction. It can be about negative influences in the life of the Querent, negativity, anger, jealousy, envy, spite. It can be about a perversion of justice or a relationship spiralling downwards, but it's important to remember that this card indicates that this negativity is coming from within someone, the Querent or someone around them. I do not interpret this card as anything demonic. It's too easy to blame an invisible entity for all our problems when we make most of our problems ourselves through carelessness, laziness and bad choices.

Next to the Magician ID, the Querent has followed someone, treated them as they would a guru only to find this person a fraud. Take care. Next to the Five of Wands, competition has taken an ugly turn, beware of sabotage and rumour. Next to either the Emperor or the Empress ID, someone is being bullied by a powerful person. Next to the Nine of Coins, there is an indication of financial matters which are out of control. Either spending is entirely too high or losses are being had in other areas. Take care to ensure you are in control of your finances.

III Dignified: it can mean troubles are about to get out of hand, or that they have been (only) temporarily delayed. The Querent needs to seriously rethink aspects of their life and how to deal with this before it comes to a head. It can indicate a relationship that has become a cycle of abuse in which neither partner feels free to walk away.

Next to the King or Queen of Wands ID, the abusive relationship could be coming from an older person, a parent or a boss. This person cannot be reasoned with, it is futile to try and change their minds. Next to the Four of Coins ID, there is an element of jealousy which is now completely out of control. It could also indicate dishonest financial manoeuvring. Next to the Star ID, the Querent or someone near them is deluding themselves into thinking that a horrible situation will get better. It hasn't in the past and it probably won't. The Querent needs to open their eyes.

THE TOWER

destruction Change

This is massive, sudden, destructive change. It can be unpleasant and not usually of the Querent's choosing. It can mean a sudden, ugly domestic shift, the discovery of some unwelcome information is imminent. It can indicate some cataclysmic event which is going to send the Querent reeling. There's little that can be done about this, by the time this card pops up whatever it is

163

that's on its way is either at hand or has already happened. It's important to remind the Querent that out of the ashes, something new will grow. What might seem like a disaster at first can actually be a blessing in disguise, though it may not immediately feel like this way.

Next to the Lovers, the Ace of Cups, the Two of Cups, it could indicate some sort of problem in the Querent's relationships. Next to the Ten of Coins ID, there could be problems at home, financially or medically. Next to the Six of Cups ID, someone from the Querent's past may make a sudden and possibly unwelcome appearance in their life.

III Dignified: this can indicate abrupt change of a lesser type or that this disaster has been delayed somewhat. What at first seems horrible will later not seem as bad as first thought. Looming consequences could possibly be avoided if steps are taken now in order to remedy the situation. It can also intensify the seriousness of the situation, again, depending on the cards around it. If the situation is intensified instead of being modified or delayed, the Querent will need to garner all their resources to weather the storm.

Next to the Six of Swords, there is an indication that the sudden change has already happened and that better times are ahead. Next to the Six of Swords ID, the problems are likely just beginning but there is a light at the end of the tunnel. Next to the Queen of Swords, the Empress, the Queen of Cups, do not despair. The Querent will receive support and help from the people around them in order to make it through a tough time. If the Tower ID appears next to Justice, it could indicate that this situation is either retribution for something the

Querent has said or done, or that someone who has done wrong will be made to pay.

THE STAR

Faith delusions

This card embodies the elements of hope and faith. It's literally like a star that guides you where you need to be. Sometimes, especially after the disaster of the Tower, the Querent is going to have to go on the idea that something good is going to happen, they just need a little faith. Keep an eye out for signs, odd coincidences. It is the possibility of getting an answer from an unexpected source. The Star can guide us from anywhere and can also indicate a person in the Querent's life who will shine a beacon or provide support during a difficult time. No matter what happens, the Querent must never give up hope. Even if their faith in their friends and family is tested (sometimes to the breaking point) the Querent must always remember to have faith in herself.

Next to the Two of Swords, a difficult decision has to be made. There may be some advantage in waiting for a moment and waiting for a sign as to which path to take. Next to the Ten of Cups or the Ten of Coins, family life and health will improve. Next to the Ace of Swords, mental clarity will lead to the Querent walking the right path.

III **Dignified:** it can indicate faith mistakenly placed, delusions of grandeur. It can indicate a lack of realistic thinking. The thing the Querent is hoping for is not going to come to fruition and it's time they admitted that to themselves. It is likely that the Querent has been lying to himself for some time now and when asked directly will admit that he knows the truth about the situation. It could be that the Querent has not done the work involved to reach their goals, it could be that the goals are simply out of reach. Realistic hope has become delusional thinking. The Querent must guard against being led by people who present themselves as being wiser than others. Be on guard for chicanery and fraud.

Next to the Eight of Swords, the Querent has (possibly deliberately) turned a blind eye towards someone or something which promised a great reward and has not lived up to that promise. Next to the Lovers (also ID) the reality of a romantic relationship may not measure up to the Querent's desires. Next to the Knight of Cups ID, the Querent has been deliberately misled by someone who seeks to gain an emotional advantage over them.

THE MOON

Deception Confusion

This card indicates deception, confusion or an inability to find your way out of the darkness. The Querent could be involved with people who employ double-speak and who avoid answering direct questions with direct answers. It can speak of depression or of mental problems. It can indicate the Querent is being lied to or scammed somehow, either in business or in their personal life. It could be that the Querent is lying to himself and needs to start seeing things more realistically. There could also be a sense of individuals who are changeable in nature. Just as the moon waxes and wanes, there are people in the Querent's life who run hot and cold, creating a confusing environment. It could simply be that these people are moody and this is their nature. It could also be an elaborate game they are playing in order to unsettle the Querent or to cause problems.

Next to the Page of Swords (especially ID), the Moon can indicate unfounded, untrue gossip or rumour being spread deliberately to cause hurt and pain. Next to the Seven of Swords (especially ID) the Querent must be careful who they trust as someone in their circle may not have their best interests at heart. Next to the Four of Cups (especially ID), too many choices have left the Querent overwhelmed and yet none of the choices is especially appealing.

III Dignified: It can indicate mental illness. There could be serious problems either with the Querent or someone close to them. It could be a conspiracy of silence in which people know the truth but are unwilling or unable to share it. This can create a sense of overwhelming confusion. There is a great deal of sadness that accompanies this card. It can indicate the feeling of being separate from others, being lost in some way. The Querent must find his way back to a happier, more joyful place.

Next to the Three of Swords (also ID) the Querent has lost a relationship of great value and the grief is overwhelming and he is in danger of slipping into a deep depression. Next to the Ten of Swords (especially ID) someone has deliberately said or done something to hurt the Querent, and the lasting effect is one of sadness and depression. Next to the Hermit, the Querent has been pulling away from their social life for some time, it would be a good idea for them to try to reconnect with the people they care about.

The Sun

warmth Strength

After coming out of the trials and tribulations of all the other Major Arcana cards, the Sun indicates a period of warmth and strength. It's a time to literally, spiritually, emotionally let the sun shine on your face and be absorbed in warmth. It's a time of celebration after a win, or after a hard time. It is a time of rest and growth. The Sun can indicate that it's time to let go of old beliefs or grudges that have been holding you back. The Querent must allow herself a time of celebration and warmth.

Next to the Six of Wands, victory is at hand and after achieving his goal, the Querent will experience an unexpected feeling of warmth and happiness. Next to the Nine Coins, a period of financial ease is at hand. Next to the Tower, what was previously thought to be disastrous will prove to be a blessing in disguise.

III Dignified: this card indicates delays but eventual victory is likely. The Querent is reminded to hang on, that things will get better. It could be that victory will not be as sweet as originally hoped for but that it will come, nonetheless. The Querent could be undergoing a trying period at the moment, but she will come out the other side stronger and better off than when she began.

Next to the Star it can indicate that ways of thinking and delusions are pointless and wishing for things that won't happen is futile. Let go of these things and see life begin. Next to the Four of Coins ID, a release from jealousy or avarice will invite a sense of calm and happiness. Next to the Five of Coins ID, accept the help that has been offered and your suffering will be lessened. Pride is of little use in this situation.

JUDGEMENT

Debt vindication

This is not just the warning of karmic debt, but the actual calling in of a debt. The Querent (or someone near them) will be asked to "pay up" so to speak, for all the things they've done. If they were the victims of someone else's actions there will be some kind of vindication. It can also be a sense of freedom and relief, of starting over after the debt has been taken care of. It can literally be a legal judgement for or against the Querent or it can be the opinion of others. Those who have been acting behind the scenes to make trouble will be exposed. The Querent's hard work and effort (or lack thereof) will be recognised.

Next to Justice ID, the decision may not go in the Querent's favour, but this is not entirely unjustified. Next to the Seven of Coins (especially ID) the Querent's lack of commitment to a project will be noted. If possible, he is advised to do as much as possible to minimise the damage. Next to the Ten of Swords (especially ID) there is the sense that someone who has deliberately hurt another will be exposed for what they are.

III Dignified: it can indicate a judgement delayed or intensified. It may or may not go in the favour of the Querent and if the judgement is harsh in nature, it could be excessively so. It can indicate a loss of face either for the Querent or for someone who has wronged them. There could be the element of public embarrassment or exposure involved. It may be that someone who has been causing trouble for the Querent will be publicly admonished. Be warned, however, taking pleasure in someone else's discomfort or punishment may invite trouble into the life of the Querent.

Next to the Queen of Swords ID, the judgement will possibly be extreme in its nature. Doors will be closed. Next to the King of Wands, the initial nature of the judgement will be harsh, but perhaps will be softened somewhat through the intervention of a sober, impartial party. Next to the Lovers, (especially ID), it could indicate that there has been an element of deception involved in this relationship and this will be exposed.

THE WORLD

Wisdom   Satisfaction

Having undergone the experiences, felt the pain, learned the lessons, the Querent has now come to the end of the Fool's journey. This is a time of calm and peace for the Querent, but we must always remember that the journey we take isn't a static one; it keeps repeating itself again and again at every stage of our lives. The Querent has learned these lessons, but there is more out there and every time they go on this journey, they bring with them more wisdom and experience. The lows aren't so low, and perhaps the highs aren't as high, but life becomes more manageable as people mature and grow. Success in a project has been reached. Maturity is at hand.

Next to the Seven of Wands, after a period of feeling embattled, the Querent has come out the other side of their journey/ordeal stronger and wiser. Next to the Nine of Wands ID, true success cannot be achieved until the Querent agrees to let go. Learning to relax and accept things as they come will lead to a better place. Next to the Six of Swords, a distressing situation is now over. It is not time to dwell on past problems, but to enjoy the peace of the moment.

III Dignified: a delay in the arrival of success or a period not as calm or as peaceful as the Querent would have hoped. Perhaps it is the case that the Querent believed that they would feel some level of satisfaction if only they could achieve a particular goal. Having reached that goal, they may find that they feel flat and apathetic. There is a light at the end of the tunnel; it just isn't here right this minute.

Next to the Seven of Cups ID, there is the sense that the Querent has too many options and refuses to see the benefits they have right in front of them. Happiness is the art of wanting what you have, not having what you want. Next to the Three of Cups, a celebration has fallen flat; it wasn't what was hoped for. Next to the Four of Swords ID, the Querent knows what they must do in order to achieve their goals but is not doing it and instead is complaining about not being where they want to be. The message is clear: do the work and reap the rewards.

SPREADS

There are as many different ways to lay cards as there are readers and in my opinion, each one of them is valid. I do not believe there is a right or wrong way to lay the cards, nor do I believe there is a right way or a wrong way to interpret the cards. There is only your way and my way, and though they may be very different, one is not necessarily better than the other. Because I think it's important for each reader to develop their own style, I will not belabour the point. I'll simply point out a few spreads which I find useful and over time, you will certainly discover and develop your own.

Different spreads can be used for a variety of reasons and situations. Though I was taught about ten different kinds of spreads, I typically use around five of them, using what I need depending on the situation or even how much time I have. The point is that as you grow in your practice, you will find ways of laying the cards that both appeal to you speak to you, and that is what's most important.

There are some people who believe that odd numbers bring good luck. For example, in the countries of former Yugoslavia, it is considered very bad luck to bring an even number of flowers as a gift to someone as even numbers of flowers are better suited to cemeteries. Odd numbers are considered good luck by some, however, this is not the case across the board. It's up to you if you feel that the number of cards you use in your spread is of importance.

Learning to read spreads takes time, so be patient with yourself. There is a subtlety and nuance to reading the parts of a person's life and recognising the characters and issues within. It takes time to see how certain cards apply to certain people and what they can indicate. Don't rush yourself. I've been reading tarot now for a long time and I still feel there's so much for me to learn.

I have seen some readers who, as they lay the cards, say something like "this crosses you, this covers you, this is your past, and this is your future..." I was taught this way, but to be perfectly honest, I've all but abandoned that. I feel that adding to the "mystique" of the reading removes the reader from the Querent and makes dialogue more difficult. I also think that one card cannot represent your future. The future, I believe, is largely unknowable and that's what makes it so wonderful. Cards can indicate future consequences of present actions, but at any moment we have the ability to change the way we live and the decisions we make which will of course, change the future.

My advice is to stay away from what I call mystical mumbo-jumbo and just read the cards.

One thing I do find important is *how* you physically lay the cards on the table. I was taught that you should turn the card over by taking hold of the long sides of the card and turning it over, (in the same way you can turn the palm of your hand from facing downwards to facing upwards or turning the pages of a book). This will not change the card from being dignified to Ill Dignified.

If you take the card off the deck and turn it over by flipping it from the bottom to the top (using the motion you'd make by turning your wrist in the motion you would whisk eggs) you actually change the card from being dignified to Ill Dignified and therefore can change the meaning of the card and hence the reading.

If a card seems odd or difficult to interpret, do not force a meaning on to it. If you are not able to recognise who or what this symbolises, simply take note of it. The meaning will likely become clear later on. Remember, if you are reading for yourself, not every card you pull is going to be about you; sometimes a card will come up which indicates the trials and tribulations of family members, friends and co-workers. The same is equally true for reading for clients. Someone may have a reading more about their partner or a friend than about themselves. I have no idea why this is, but it is useless to attempt to extrapolate a meaning for a card if it simply doesn't apply to that person at that particular moment.

If at any time, a card in a spread seems strange or out of place (and they will from time to time) it is perfectly acceptable to pull two or three more cards from the top of the deck and lay them next to the card you find perplexing. Sometimes this can help to clarify things. Often, I find that cards that seem strange or out of place may not be clear for several days. For example: I read for myself some time ago and saw the Six of

Swords ID, generally read as a card about the end of troubles, heading into calmer waters. Since at that time I was having no particular turbulence in my life, it held no meaning for me. Later that day, a friend of mine told me a story about how her relationship was improving after a difficult time. I hadn't even known that she had been having issues with her partner so it came as a surprise to me. Here it was, calmer waters.

Here are a few spreads you can use in your practice.

ONE CARD

Though it may seem strange, laying one card can actually be a powerful tool when asking a yes or no question. You can also use the one card spread as a tool for contemplation. In the past, and especially when I was learning tarot, I pulled one card every morning and read about it. Often I thought the card had no meaning at all to me personally, but throughout the course of the day I would often be surprised to find that the card touched upon a story a friend would related to me, something I would see or hear during my day or something I would read in the newspaper. At any given moment, any card can apply to either you or someone you know.

Ask the Querent to form a question to which there can be only a yes or no answer. For example, a question such as "How can I save my relationship?" isn't particularly useful for a one card spread, and I would hasten to point out that cards cannot give you the answers on how to improve your life. They can help you make decisions, but they do not make decisions for you or tell you how things are going to be.

THREE CARDS

Laying three cards in a row can be used to look at events in terms of past, present and future, or simply to get a sense of how things are going. From left to right, the first card can represent the past, the second can represent the present and the third can represent the future. I tend to read the cards in tandem, not as isolated cards representing isolated time periods, but as a whole picture of a current (or past) situation. Getting a sense of reading combinations takes time and practice, but in my opinion, it's well worth it.

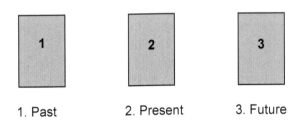

1. Past   2. Present   3. Future

THE INVERTED PYRAMID

The Pyramid is a spread I use when I want to get an overall sense of the life of the Querent. (I often use this spread when doing a quick reading for myself.) I do not ascribe any particular significance or meaning to the position of cards but you are certainly welcome to do so if it would make your reading more complete. Simply put, the Inverted Pyramid is a pyramid of cards, six in the first row, five in the second, four in the third, and so on until you have one card at the bottom.

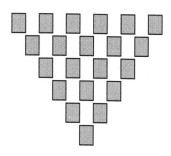

If you prefer, you can use the spread "the right way up" so the peak of the pyramid (the row with one card) is at the top.

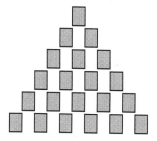

I use this spread to get a sense of all the factors that are involved with the life of the Querent. Our lives are made up of so many parts, family, friends, work, neighbours, the towns we live in, our health, finances, our hobbies, wishes and desires, that I find the Inverted Pyramid a nice way of getting sense of everything that makes up our daily lives. Again, I tend to look at the cards in combinations, not as individual cards, but individual cards can be significant as well.

THE CYCLE

The Cycle is a spread that I was taught can be used once a year to indicate what the challenges and issues of the coming year will bring. I think you can safely use it more often than once a year, but it does give a nice continuity to the idea of the seasons. The cycle is twelve cards laid out in a square, three in each "corner". Each corner represents a season, usually with the top left corner being spring, and then in a clockwise direction, summer, autumn and winter.

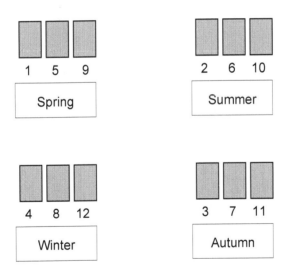

1 5 9	2 6 10
Spring	Summer

4 8 12	3 7 11
Winter	Autumn

(If you are reading the card in autumn, for example, the top left corner can be autumn and the subsequent clock-wise corners can be winter, spring and summer.)

You can lay the cards one in each corner as though you were dealing cards to other people to play bridge, or if you prefer, you can lay all three cards in each corner before moving on to the next corner.

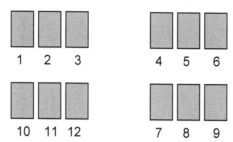

It's up to you. Again, this spread requires the ability to read combinations of cards or to see the bigger picture as it will be tiresome and pointless to read one card at a time.

X

Laying the cards in the form of an X (see below) can be another useful way to have an overview of the Querent's current situation.

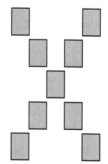

It is similar to laying the cards in a circle or a pyramid. Looking at the cards diagonally can give the reader a new slant and again, reading the cards in groups or combinations does not necessarily mean only cards that are physically next to one another. Look for themes within the cards, such as jealousy, love, strife, victory and read from there.

THE CLOCK

The Clock is a spread that can be used to look at the people and issues surrounding the Querent. Simply put, it is twelve cards in a circle in the same positions as the numbers on a clock, with a thirteenth card in the centre. I use this spread to begin a dialogue with the Querent about the various parts of their lives, people they know, issues and challenges they have to face.

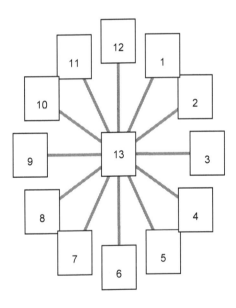

You may have noticed that I have omitted to include the Celtic Cross as a spread. It is true that this is a very common spread and is widely used, but I must confess I do not have a fondness for it. I dislike the way the

Celtic Cross is read, each card representing one definite part of a Querent's life (Past, Present, Future, House, etc). I prefer to read the cards in tandem, looking for recurring themes and reading them in terms of cards that compliment, enhance or mitigate one another, rather than as separate, discrete occurrences. If you are interested in learning the Celtic Cross, there is plenty of excellent information about it available in other books and on the internet.

Now we come to the end of The Open Minded Tarot. I wish you all the best in your studies and hope that you will find your work with the Tarot as fulfilling and fascinating a journey as I have found mine to be.

Best wishes,

Kate Ross

ACKNOWLEDGEMENTS

I wish to thank my friends and family for their patience and encouragement over the years and while writing this book. To Martin for his generosity and kindness, (Děkuji!). To Luna Apollonio, the talented young artist who did the artwork used in the book, I thank you. Luna can be reached at lunaapollonioart@gmail.com. To Chloe Johnson, for her friendship over the years and for inspiring this book in the first place. Most of all, I'd like to extend my sincere and profound thanks to Gail for her incredibly hard work and amazing ideas. I am blessed and thankful to have you for a friend and collaborator.

66459032R00103

Made in the USA
Lexington, KY
14 August 2017